AMERICAN INDIAN CONTRIBUTIONS TO THE WORLD

Trade, Transportation, and Warfare

EMORY DEAN KEOKE

KAY MARIE PORTERFIELD

Facts On File, Inc.

Trade, Transportation, and Warfare

Maps on pages 126–136 © 2005 by Carl Waldman
Maps on pages 3, 54, 137–138 © 2005 by Facts On File, Inc.

Facts On File, Inc.
132 West 31st Street
New York NY 10001

Library of Congress Cataloging-in-Publication Data
Keoke, Emory Dean.
  American Indian contributions to the world. Trade, transportation, and warfare /
Emory Dean Keoke and Kay Marie Porterfield.
     v. cm.
  Includes bibliographical references and index.
  Contents: Traders of North America — Traders of Mesoamerica and South America
— Transportation on water — Transportation on land — Roads, trails, and bridges —
Sports and games — Armor and weapons — Military strategy — Military contributions
— Diplomacy and government — Ancient cultures of the Americas.
  ISBN 0-8160-5395-2
  1. Indians—Commerce—Juvenile literature. 2. Indians—Warfare—Juvenile
literature. 3. Indian roads—Juvenile literature. 4. Indians—Boats—Juvenile literature.
[1. Indians—Commerce. 2. Indians—Warfare. 3. Indians—Transportation.]
I. Porterfield, Kay Marie. II. Title.
E59.C59K46 2005
970.004'97—dc22   2003025977

Text design by Erika K. Arroyo
Cover design by Cathy Rincon
Illustrations by Sholto Ainslie

Printed in the United States of America

VB FOF 10 9 8 7 6 5 4 3 2 1

This book is printed on acid-free paper.

For our grandchildren:
Jason Keoke, Gwendolyn Z. McPherson,
Matthew Geboe, Jr., and Jonathan Ward McPherson;
and in memory of Merrill W. Bowen, Jr.

⬚ *Note on Photos* ⬚

Many of the illustrations and photographs used in this book are old, historical images. The quality of the prints is not always up to current standards because in many cases the originals are from old or poor quality negatives or the originals are damaged. The content of the illustrations, however, made their inclusion important despite problems in reproduction.

CONTENTS

AUTHORS' NOTE

At least 800 unique tribes, or bands, of Indian people lived in the Americas at the time Europeans first arrived there in 1492. A tribe is a community or group of families who share the same culture, or way of living. The things that make up a culture can range from clothing and housing styles to ways of singing or praying. They include how people make and decorate the objects that they use in their daily lives. Tribal members speak the same language. Sometimes the language they speak is similar to the one that their neighbors speak. It could also be very different. A list of tribes of Indian people is located at the end of this book.

American Indians were and continue to be skilled at adapting to the places where they live. From the start, the features of the land where Indian people lived and the plants and animals that they found there influenced their way of life. Their cultures were also shaped by the climate and by neighboring tribes. Tribes that lived in similar regions developed many of the same ways of doing things. For example, they used many of the same medicines and developed similar styles of art. The geographical regions where similar tribes live are called culture areas. The list of tribes at the end of the book is divided into culture areas. Maps of these culture areas are also located at the back of this book. The maps contain the names of tribes that live in these areas.

Over time tribes and their cultures change. Some of the tribes mentioned in this book existed hundreds or thousands of years ago, but they do not exist as groups today. The people themselves did not vanish. Their language changed along with their way of doing things. Sometimes they moved. Sometimes they became part of other tribes.

Other tribal groups, such as the Maya of Mesoamerica, have ancient beginnings and continue to exist today. A glossary of ancient cultures that are mentioned in this book is located on page 113. Here readers will find a short explanation of when these ancient people lived and where they lived. Maps at the end of the book show the location of these ancient peoples as well.

The cultures of the first Americans were so varied and their accomplishments were so many that it would be impossible to write everything about them in one book or even a series of books. The authors apologize in advance for anything in this book that might offend any tribe or band of American Indians. There has been no intention to speak on behalf of any tribe or to pretend knowledge in the ways of all Indian people.

INTRODUCTION

Indian peoples have lived in the Americas for at least 15,000 years. Many scientists believe that the very first Americans came from Asia, traveling over a land bridge that emerged from the sea several times during the Ice Age. This strip of land, called Beringia, connected what is now Siberia with what is now Alaska between 15,000 and 7,000 B.C. (some believe even earlier). Other scientists think that the first Americans might have traveled in boats as well, settling along what is now the Alaska coastline. After they arrived in the Americas, Indians continued to travel. By at least 10,500 B.C. they were living in what is now Monte Verde, in Chile— about 11,000 miles from Beringia.

To accomplish this, Indian people worked together to make certain that everyone had food to eat, a place to live, and was safe from danger. Cooperation and sharing allowed them to survive and to thrive in the Americas. Good relationships with other people were, and continue to be, important in American Indian cultures.

Families were the smallest group to which Indian people belonged. From the Inuit of the Arctic to the Inca, who established a huge empire in South America, family life came first. American Indian families were not only made up of a mother, father, and children. Grandparents, aunts, uncles, and cousins all looked after other family members. Often they lived together.

Many families joined to form small bands and larger tribes. The people who belonged to these bands and tribes spoke the same language, shared the same beliefs, and had the same ways of doing things. By connecting with others, families could more easily hunt and gather. They were also better able to defend themselves against natural dangers and human enemies. Bands and tribes are considered societies. Societies are groups of people who depend on one another.

As American Indians began to move over the land, they settled in different areas with unique resources. Bands and tribes traded some of the resources that they had with other Indians in exchange for resources that they needed. By cooperating with other tribes and sharing resources, they could improve their lives. As Indian people taught themselves to farm and make pottery and other items, they had more things to trade. They began developing closer relationships with other tribes.

In order to trade, Indians had to travel. Sometimes they traveled over great distances. They made many kinds of boats and used them to go from place to place over rivers and the ocean. They created trails along the easiest land routes from place to place. Some groups of Indian people in Mesoamerica and South America built roads. By the time Europeans arrived in the Americas, Indians had developed a network of river routes, trails, and roads that connected them to other groups of Indians.

They used these roads for visiting as well as trading. Indian people gathered with people of neighboring tribes to play sports as well. Sometimes sports were used as a way to settle differences.

Most groups of American Indians preferred to talk through their differences with other tribes, but sometimes conflicts arose that resulted in fighting. Indians throughout the Americas invented many types of armor and protective clothing to keep themselves from being injured in battle. They used much of what they had learned from hunting when they fought with enemy tribes. They also came up with new ways to fight and to defend themselves. Many American Indian military techniques are still used by soldiers today.

Indian tribes had ways to govern themselves. In most cases, the oldest and most respected members of family groups chose the leaders of most American Indian tribes. They did this in council meetings where they shared their ideas and came to a group decision. As tribes grew in size, some developed more formal ways for choosing leaders and making decisions for the entire group. The Iroquois, an alliance of six tribes of the Northeast, established a constitution that contained many elements of democracy. The Aztec in Mesoamerica and the Inca in Peru formed empires, large territories that were governed by a ruler who had complete authority. The Aztec and the Inca also developed laws, formal rules for how group members were expected to behave.

American Indian tribes were many, and they were unique. Tribes had many different beliefs and developed many different customs, or ways of life, that were based on the environment in which they lived. Indians of the Americas spoke more than 1,000 different languages at the time of European contact. Indian people throughout the Americas speak about 700 languages today. (Researchers believe that several tribes of Indians who live in the Amazon rain forest have not had any contact with non-Indians, so that number may be higher.)

Today in the United States 562 Indian tribes are recognized as sovereign nations by the U.S. government. The U.S. government does not yet recognize more than 250 more Indian tribes. Many of these tribes have petitioned for recognition from the U.S. government. Despite their diversity, members of American Indian tribes still value their connection with other American Indian people today.

Traders of North America

Early Indians who lived in North America needed stones that could be easily shaped into knives and spear points. They obtained these special stones from quarries that were located many miles from where they lived. Although they could have traveled to these quarries, it is far more likely that they traded with other Indians for flint, obsidian, and chert stones.

About 13,000 years ago Paleo-Indians began chiseling flint from a quarry located in what is now the Panhandle region of Texas. Flint points made from this Texas stone that are 11,000 years old have been found in eastern New Mexico. Other Paleo-Indians quarried stone in what are now Kentucky and Ohio. Weapon points made from this stone have been found in what is now Pennsylvania. These points are from 9,000 to 11,000 years old. Flint that originated in what is now Ontario, Canada, has been found as far west as Saskatchewan and Alberta.

LONG-DISTANCE TRADE

About 5,000 years ago American Indians began trading over much longer distances. They traded raw materials that were plentiful in their region to people who could not otherwise obtain them. Indians of the southern California coast exchanged asphalt from natural tar pits for hides. American Indians traded shells, turquoise, and soapstone used for making bowls. They also traded pigments used for making paint, shark teeth, turtle shells, medicines, and dishes made of horn. Indians traded crops they had grown. Some tribes began specializing in making trade items, such as pottery, jewelry, and art.

1

▲▽▲▽▲▽▲▽▲▽▲▽▲▽▲▽▲▽▲▽▲▽▲

SHELL MONEY

Indian people of Southern California were such accomplished traders that in about 1000 B.C. they began shaping and drilling shell disks that they used as money. Pomo people made the shells uniform in thickness so that when they were strung, they could either measure or count them to determine their value.

▽▲▽▲▽▲▽▲▽▲▽▲▽▲▽▲▽▲▽▲▽▲▽

The Inuit who lived near the Coppermine River in the Arctic traded copper and soapstone with other bands. Inuit traders also sailed across the Bering Strait to trade with the people of Siberia. Some archaeologists, scientists who study the past, believe Inuit trade with Siberia began 3,000 years ago. North American Indians who lived in the Southwest traded items that originated deep inside Mesoamerica. Indians of the Southeast traded for goods from Indians who lived on Caribbean islands.

Goods often changed hands many times before arriving at their final destinations hundreds and even thousands of miles away. California coastal Indians had more shells than they could use. They wanted pottery and cloth, but travel to what is now Arizona to obtain them from the Hohokam people, whose culture arose in about 300 B.C., was not practical. Instead, they traded their surplus shells with the Mojave Indians, who lived closer to them, for red ocher pigment and hide clothing.

The Mojave used some of the California shells to trade for cloth and pottery with the Hohokam. They kept some of the cloth and pots and traded the rest with the California coastal Indians. Because the Mojave acted as brokers, or go-betweens, for tribes that lived on either side of them, they made the trading network larger.

▲▽▲▽▲▽▲▽▲▽▲▽▲▽▲▽▲▽▲▽▲▽▲▽

BUILDING GOOD RELATIONSHIPS

Many Indian people thought of trading as an exchange of gifts of equal value. Generosity earned respect and honor in tribal communities. Trading also gave Indian people a chance to build good relationships with other tribes.

▽▲▽▲▽▲▽▲▽▲▽▲▽▲▽▲▽▲▽▲▽▲▽

Trading did not stop there. The Hohokam exchanged their surplus shells with southern Plains Indians for buffalo hides. The farther the shells moved from the ocean, the scarcer they became. With each trade, they increased in value. By between 500 and 200 B.C. North American Indians had established a vital trade network throughout North America.

NORTH AMERICAN INDIAN TRADING CENTERS

North American Indians developed several major trading centers. The earliest of these were the cities built by the Mound Builders in the Mississippi and Ohio River Valleys, including the Adena and Hopewell people. Hohokam and Anasazi cities of the desert Southwest were also important early trading communities.

Later, the Mandan and Hidatsa created a trading center on the Knife River in North Dakota near an old Paleo-Indian flint quarry. Indians who lived on the Dalles of the Columbia River in the

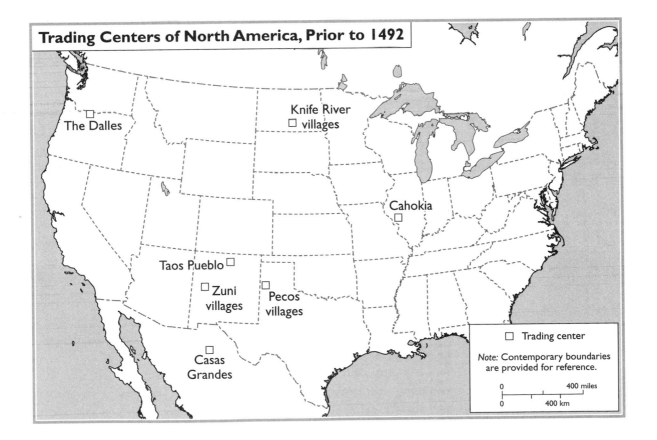

Trading Centers of North America, Prior to 1492

The Dalles

Knife River
villages

Cahokia

Taos Pueblo
Zuni
villages
Pecos
villages

Casas
Grandes

☐ Trading center

Note: Contemporary boundaries are provided for reference.

0   400 miles
0   400 km

The Adena traded items like this pipe bowl for raw materials, such as shells and precious stones. They used these raw materials to make art objects. *(Library of Congress, Prints and Photographs Division [LC-USZ62-049401])*

Northwest developed another regional trade center. The Huron of the Northeast also traded with many tribes.

Traders of the Southeast

The Adena and Hopewell were farmers of the Mississippi and Ohio River Valleys who traded extra food with neighboring groups of Indians. Both the Adena and Hopewell buried their dead with jewelry and beautiful objects beneath large mounds of earth. They needed shells, precious stones, and other material to make burial items, so they traded pottery with other Indians. They also traded finished luxury goods, such as copper and stone ear spools (a type of earring), and carved stone smoking pipes.

Indian traders traveled the rivers to obtain goods from the Adena and Hopewell, whose cities became centers of exchange. The visiting traders brought copper from the shores of Lake Superior, mica from the Appalachian Mountains, and alligator teeth and conch shells from what is now Florida. They carried yellow obsidian from the Yellowstone River in the Rocky Mountains. Adena and Hopewell traders also traveled in order to trade with other groups of Indians.

In about A.D. 1000 the Mississippian city of Cahokia, which was located across the river from what is now St. Louis, became a center of trade. Cahokia was the largest precontact city in North America. The Mississippian city dwellers made flint-bladed hoes and stone axes that they traded with nearby farmers for food. They traded salt from deposits nearby. Artists made jewelry and carvings that they traded with people from far away for freshwater pearls and shells.

Traders of the Southwest

The Hohokam and the Anasazi traded cotton cloth, pottery, jewelry, and turquoise (a blue-green stone) for obsidian from the northern part of Arizona and the area near what is now Sonora, Mexico. They also traded with brokers to obtain shells from the Gulf of California as well as bells and other goods that originated in Mesoamerica. Anasazi culture flourished in what are now New Mexico, Arizona, Utah, and Colorado from about 350 B.C. to A.D. 1450. The Anasazi are considered to be the ancestors of today's Pueblo Indians.

The Hohokam and Anasazi mined turquoise at what are now Kingman and Morenci, Arizona. Anasazi Indians also mined turquoise in what is now Colorado, and at Chaco Canyon and Cerillos in what is now New Mexico. Turquoise from Cerillos has been found in Aztec (Mexica) cities in central Mexico. Stones that the Anasazi mined in Chaco Canyon were traded as far as Chichén Itzá, a Maya city on the Yucatán Peninsula. The Aztec moved to the Valley of Mexico in about A.D. 1100. Maya culture flourished in the lowlands of what is now Mexico.

▲▽▲▽▲▽▲▽▲▽▲▽▲▽▲▽▲▽▲▽▲▽▲▽▲▽▲

PARROT BREEDING
The people of Casas Grandes built pens to house parrots and macaws. They raised them for their feathers, which they traded to the Hohokam and Anasazi. The people of Casas Grandes learned to breed birds from Mesoamericans who valued rare and brightly colored feathers more than they valued gold.

▼▲▽▲▽▲▽▲▽▲▽▲▽▲▽▲▽▲▽▲▽▲▽▲▽▲▽

The largest southwestern trade center was Casas Grandes (Big Houses), a city in what is now northern Mexico about 50 miles from the Texas border. The people there built huge warehouses to store goods from metal bells and large and small shells to fancy cloth that they had obtained from Mesoamerican traders far to the south. They

Nampeyo, a Hopi potter, displays some of the pottery she made in this 1901 photograph. People of the Southwest made pottery to trade at large fairs. Pueblo people still make and sell pottery today. *(National Archives and Records Administration at College Park/Photo No. NWDNS-79-HPS-6-3277)*

traded these with people who lived to the north, including the Hohokam and Anasazi, for turquoise and other precious stones that they exchanged with Mesoamerican traders.

Later the Pueblo people of the Southwest continued to trade obsidian, turquoise, cloth, and painted pottery with other tribes. They traded shell beads that they obtained from Indians on the Gulf of Mexico with Plains tribes for buffalo hides and leather clothing. They also traded corn, beans, and squash to hunting tribes.

People of the Zuni Pueblo traded salt. Taos Pueblo in what is now northern New Mexico and Pecos Pueblo near what is the New Mexico/Texas border held large trade fairs with the Comanche and Apache of the southern Great Plains.

Traders of the Plains

By the 1500s the Mandan and Hidatsa people had migrated up the Missouri River to settle on the Knife River. Paleo-Indians had quarried flint nearby thousands of years before. Because this flint flaked to a very sharp edge, it was still in high demand among northern Plains Indians. They traveled to the Knife River villages to trade for it as well as for corn, beans, squash, and tobacco that Mandan and Hidatsa farmers raised. In exchange they gave the Knife River traders dried meat, hide clothing, and buffalo robes.

Two major trade routes crossed at the Knife River villages, so the Mandan and Hidatsa became brokers. They traded copper from the Great Lakes, shells from both the Pacific Northwest and the Gulf of Mexico, and obsidian from what is now Wyoming. They held large trade fairs that drew Indians from throughout the central Plains, including the Crow, Cheyenne, and Lakota/Nakota/Dakota. Visiting Indian traders erected as many as 300 tipis around the villages during the fairs.

Indians of the northern and southern Great Plains traded hides for

▲▽▲▽▲▽▲▽▲▽▲▽▲▽▲▽▲▽▲▽▲▽▲▽▲▽▲▽▲▽▲

SIGN LANGUAGE

Many Indian tribes of the Great Plains used a system of hand signals, or gestures, to communicate with other traders who did not know their language. The sign language that they invented was made up of more than 1,000 distinct gestures. Indians also used sign language to relay information during hunting or raiding parties when silence was critical. The Nez Perce of the Plateau and the Ute of the Great Basin also used sign language.

▽▲▽▲▽▲▽▲▽▲▽▲▽▲▽▲▽▲▽▲▽▲▽▲▽▲▽▲▽▲▽

pipestone that had been quarried from southwest Minnesota. Pipestone, which is sometimes called catlinite, is a soft, easily carved red rock. Indian people used it for making pipe bowls and figurines. Catlinite was traded as far east as what is now New York State.

Traders of the Northwest

The Dalles of the Columbia River between what are now Washington State and Oregon attracted Indian traders from throughout the Northwest and the Plateau regions. Every summer traders came to this area bringing goods. The Columbia River people traded salmon and fish oil. They also acted as brokers for goods from nearby areas. They traded beaver and sea otter pelts, canoes, blankets, mountain sheep wool, seal oil, nuts, berries, and baskets. In addition they traded abalone and dentalium shells from the California coast. They traded these goods for deer and buffalo hides, dried deer and buffalo meat, pemmican (dried meat mixed with fat and berries), and furs. After the Spaniards reintroduced the horse to North America, they traded for horses. Trade goods from The Dalles have been found as far away as Alaska, southern California, and Missouri.

Traders of the Northeast

The Huron, or Wyandot, were the most active traders in the Northeast. Huron farmers lived in what is now central Ontario in Canada before contact. They grew a surplus of corn that they pounded into cornmeal. Then they traded cornmeal to tribes to the north for moose hides, furs, fish, and winter clothing that had been embroidered with porcupine quills. The Huron also served as brokers for other groups of Indians, trading corn, tobacco, and hemp fiber from other farming tribes for fish and furs.

This photograph of a Lakota Sioux Woman in traditional dress was taken in 1925. The designs on the top and sleeves of her dress are made with dentalium shells from the Pacific coast, half a continent away. People of the Plains traded for dentalium shells long before Europeans arrived. After contact some women began making their dresses from wool trade cloth as this woman has, rather than from hides. *(National Archives and Records Administration Central Plains Region/Photograph No. NRE-75-PT(PHO)-15)*

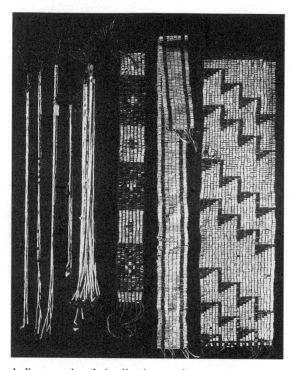

Indian people of the Northeast often strung wampum into belts to record treaties. Early colonists used wampum for money. *(National Archives and Records Administration at College Park/Photograph No. NWDNS-106-IN-18A)*

The Iroquois, a confederacy made up of the Oneida, Mohawk, Cayuga, Onondaga, Seneca, and later the Tuscarora tribes, lived in what is now New York State. They, too, were farmers who developed a large trade network with other Indian tribes, including the Algonquian speakers in the Northeast. Their trade network rivaled that of the Huron.

Algonquian-speaking tribes who lived on the coast of northeastern North America made beads from shells. Their word for these beads was *wampum*. The oldest wampum found by archaeologists, scientists who study the past, was made in about 2500 B.C. To make wampum, Indians cut shells into cylinders. Next they polished them and drilled the centers with stone drill bits. Wampum was made in two colors—white from whelk shells and purple from quahog (clam) shells, which were scarcer than whelk.

Algonquian-speaking tribes traded wampum to neighboring tribes, including the Iroquois, who wove the beads into belts as a way to record oral agreements. At times American Indians also used wampum belts as a way to record and send messages. Eastern tribes traded wampum and tobacco with the Chippewa (Anishinabe) for copper from the southern shore of Lake Superior.

COLONIAL MONEY

Metal coins were scarce in the early colonies, so European Americans used wampum for money. After they introduced metal drill bits to the Narragansett and Pequot, these tribes began mass-producing wampum beads. Wampum remained legal tender in the colonies until the late 1600s. It was used on the frontiers until the mid-1700s. Colonists made counterfeit wampum by dyeing white shell beads purple to double their value.

TRADE WITH EUROPEANS

When Christopher Columbus landed in Hispaniola in the Caribbean in 1492, his ship was met by more than 120 canoes carrying Indians bringing fish, spices, and bread made from cassava root. They were following their custom of trade by exchanging gifts. Columbus and his men traded glass beads to the Indians in return for information about where to find gold. Later conquistadores traveled throughout North America looking for gold. The French, British, and Dutch

▲▼

A FAIR TRADE?

People give value to something based on the usefulness of the item and their need for it. When people need an item, they are willing to pay more for it than if they do not need it. The scarcer an item is, the more value people assign to it. For example, a stamp is only a small piece of sticky paper. When it is used for mailing letters it grows in value to a few cents. If it is a rare stamp, it becomes worth thousands of dollars to a collector because it is scarce.

When the first Europeans in the Americas traded glass beads, Indian people assumed that they were very rare because they had not seen them before. As experienced traders, they knew that rare things have a high value. They also believed that they had more than enough gold and land to share with a small number of Europeans. It seemed like a fair trade.

The Europeans did not tell the Indians that they planned on shipping glass beads to the Americas by the ton. Nei-ther did they tell the Indian people that they wanted every bit of gold in the Americas because it was rare in Europe. They did not explain that they intended to claim all of the land in the Americas for European monarchs, because land in Europe had become scarce as well.

The beads on this leather pouch are made from glass. From the first European contact, non-Indians traded glass beads to Indians for furs and land. Before Indians used beads to decorate clothing and leather bags, they used dyed porcupine quills. (Marius Barbeau/National Archives of Canada/Photograph No. PA-175385/National Museums of Canada Collection)

▼▲

The dress worn by this Havasupai girl in 1900 is made from calico, printed cotton cloth. Non-Indians traded patterned cloth to Indians. *(National Archives and Records Administration at College Park/Photo No. NWDNS-79-HPS-6-1680)*

arrived in the Northeast looking for land and ways to make money. At first, like Columbus, they used trade in order to get what they wanted.

The Spanish conquistadores who followed Columbus began taking control of the Pueblo trade network as soon as they arrived in the Southwest. They introduced their own trade items as a way to gain the trust of the southern Plains Indians, including the Apache. By the middle of the 1600s the conquistadores were capturing the Apache and sending them to Mexico to work as slaves in Spanish mines.

Large fur trading companies, like the Northwest Company and the Hudson Bay Company, built empires of wealth on Indian trade networks. They traded guns and gunpowder for beaver, mink,

▲▽▲▽▲▽▲▽▲▽▲▽▲▽▲▽▲▽▲▽▲▽▲▽▲▽

SMALLPOX

Trade with Europeans brought smallpox to the Great Plains. The disease swept through the Knife River village in waves in 1781, 1801, 1837, and 1856. The Hidatsa, Mandan, and Arikara numbered about 7,000 before 1837. In 1837 as many as 5,000 smallpox-related deaths occurred in these tribes.

▽▲▽▲▽▲▽▲▽▲▽▲▽▲▽▲▽▲▽▲▽▲▽▲▽

fox, and bear furs. In addition to guns, the Europeans traded metal traps and cooking pots, mirrors, awls, metal needles, and glass beads.

In the 1700s fur traders from the Northwest Company and the Hudson Bay began offering European trade goods for furs at the Knife River fairs. Soon the Indian traders began brokering horses, guns, and metal items, such as knives and cooking pots, to neighboring tribes

This photograph of Mistahi Maskawa (Big Bear), a Cree chief, trading furs at Fort Pitt in the Northwest Territories of Canada was taken in 1884. Mistahi Maskawa is the fourth standing man from the left. *(O. B. Buell/National Archives of Canada/Photograph No. PA-118768)*

for Europeans in exchange for furs. The French traders renamed the fairs *rendezvous*.

By 1792 Europeans discovered that the Columbia River basin in the Northwest was rich in otter and beaver furs that they could trade with China at great profit. As they had on the Plains, the Europeans also brought both trade goods and disease. Many Indians died. By 1810, less than 20 years after the European contact, the fur trading on the Columbia River was controlled by the French.

North American Indians supported themselves by hunting, fishing, gathering, and farming. They did not depend on trade to feed their families before they traded with Europeans. Economic independence of this sort is called self-sufficiency. Indians who hunted furs for the Europeans had little time to spend hunting for food or farming. As more of their land was taken, they became more and more dependent on European trade to survive.

Fur traders encouraged Indians to kill more and more fur-bearing animals. They traded metal traps to make the work easier. The more pelts the Indians provided, the less the trappers paid for them, since they were no longer scarce. Indian trappers had to kill even more animals in order to make a living. The balance of self-sufficiency and trade that had been a way of life for North American Indians for thousands of years had disappeared.

TIME LINE	
1000 B.C.	California coastal Indians begin making shell money.
1000 B.C.	The Inuit of the Arctic begin trade with the people of Siberia.
500 B.C.	Adena people of the Ohio Valley establish a vast trade network.
300–350 B.C.	The Hohokam and Anasazi people create trade centers in the Southwest.
A.D. 1000	Cahokia becomes a major trade center in the Mississippi Valley.
A.D. 1550	Mandan and Hidatsa people hold trade fairs in what is now North Dakota.

2

Traders of Mesoamerica and South America

Thousands of years before contact with Europeans, Indians of Mesoamerica and South America exchanged surplus goods for things that they needed or wanted. At first their trade resembled that of the North American Indians. That changed with the birth of large cities, city-states, and empires.

The rulers of these cities and the nobles who served as their assistants needed a way to show their power and wealth to the people they governed. By wearing luxury goods such as fancy jewelry or clothing and owning art that came from far away, rulers and nobles made sure that everyone knew how important they were. The rare and beautiful things that they owned were symbols of their status, or rank in society. As the demand for luxury goods grew, empires expanded and the business of trading became an established profession in Mesoamerica and parts of South America. In addition to trading goods, the people of Mesoamerica and South America exchanged ideas, styles of artistic expression, and technology.

OLMEC TRADERS

The Olmec, whose culture arose in the Yucatán Peninsula of what is now Mexico in about 1700 B.C., were the first Mesoamerican traders. Even before the Olmec cities of La Venta and Laguna de los Cerros grew to a large size, the people who lived there were trading partners.

The Olmec are known for the sculptures they made from basalt, a volcanic rock. This one is of a wrestler. (© Philip Baird www.anthroarcheart.org)

The people of La Venta, which was close to the seacoast, traded salt to other Olmec people. Because their city was also near the lowland jungles, the people had access to many rubber trees. They made extra items from rubber to use as trade goods, such as rubber balls and rubber-covered cloth. Sometimes they traded bricks of processed rubber that their customers used to make things. They also traded shells and salt.

The people of Laguna de los Cerros, which was near the mountains, paid for these goods with basalt. This is a type of stone used to make *manos* and *metates* for grinding corn. A mano is a hand-held grinding stone. A metate is a flat stone that is shaped to hold the corn. The Olmec used basalt to make huge statues and as a building material. The people of the mountains also traded obsidian and jade, a green stone that the Olmec used for carving small statues and making jewelry.

As the cities grew, the Olmec began trading with Indian people who lived long distances away. They traded conch shells and stingray spines as far as the Zapotec city of Monte Albán in the Valley of Oaxaca in order to obtain mirrors of polished magnetite. The Olmec also traded with people who lived in what is now Honduras to obtain chocolate. They traded with the people of the Valley of Mexico as well. The goods that the Olmec traded included dyes, incense, and medicines. They also traded jaguar skins, feathers, turtle shell drums, shark teeth, and pottery.

The Olmec expanded their rubber trade throughout Mesoamerica and, through Mesoamerican brokers, to parts of the North American Southwest. In addition to trading rubber, the Olmec taught Mesoamerican Indians to play a ball game that they invented using rubber balls. Indians of the Southwest also played this game. The design of Olmec pottery, their mathematical system, and their writing system spread throughout Mesoamerica as a result of trade.

MAYA TRADERS

The Maya traded among themselves over land and river routes for many hundreds of years. Between A.D. 600 and A.D. 900 they began trading over the ocean. Maya culture flourished in what is now Mexico starting in about 1500 B.C. Maya ocean trading first began near Cozumel on the east coast of what is now Mexico and in what is now Belize. The traders' first voyages were short ones, mostly to an island about 18 miles off the coast.

Three hundred years later they had established several seacoast trading ports and were trading throughout the Caribbean. The earliest and most important seaport was Cerritos in what is now northern Belize where the Maya built a seawall to form an artificial harbor. This port connected the Caribbean trade routes with river routes to the southern Maya lowlands. The Maya located other trade centers along the coast as well. They built docks and piers in these ports. They also built lighthouses to warn sailors of dangerous rocks near the surface of the sea.

The Maya who lived on the coast traded shells, shark teeth, and stingray spines to inland cities many hundreds of miles away. They also traded salt. Agricultural people living inland needed salt to meet their nutritional requirements and to preserve meat. The salt beds of the northern Yucatán had enough salt so that the Maya salt traders could ship thousands of tons of it to the lowlands. The people of the lowland jungles traded cotton, spices, feathers, and jaguar pelts in return.

Maya seacoast traders obtained cacao seeds, from which chocolate is made. They served as brokers, trading these goods with people

MAYA SEA TRADERS

In 1502 Christopher Columbus encountered Maya traders on his fourth voyage off the coast of Honduras. In his book, *Historia de las Indias,* Bartolomé de Las Casas, reported that their canoe was a huge one, as long as a galley (a Spanish ship) and eight feet wide. A palm matting structure in the middle of the dugout kept women, children, and the goods dry. Each canoe contained about 25 men. "They had in it much clothing of the kind they weave of cotton in this land, such as cloth woven with many designs and colors . . . knives of flint, swords of very strong wood . . . and foodstuffs of the country," he wrote.

▲▽▲▽▲▽▲▽▲▽▲▽▲▽▲▽▲▽▲▽▲▽▲▽▲▽▲

MAYA SHOPPING MALLS

Maya people who lived in cities shopped for food, clothing, and other things that they needed at open-air markets. As Maya cities grew, suburbs sprung up around them. Each suburb had its own small market, much like the strip malls in modern cities.

▼▲▼▲▼▲▼▲▼▲▼▲▼▲▼▲▼▲▼▲▼▲▼▲▼▲▼

who lived in the highlands of what is now Guatemala, 500 miles away, for obsidian, basalt, and jade.

The Maya also traded honey, cotton, fish, and tobacco. They traded amber, feathers, coral, and semiprecious stones, including jadeite and serpentine, that were used for making jewelry. The Maya traded volcanic ash and lime that was used to make plaster and concrete. In addition they manufactured trade goods, including beautifully woven cloth, bark paper, and stone manos and metates for grinding corn.

The Maya trade network stretched thousands of miles. Pyrite mirrors and macaw feathers from Maya traders have even been found in the southwest desert of North America. Archaeologists have also found turquoise from northern Mexico and the North American desert southwest in the ruins of Maya cities.

By the time the Spanish conquistadores arrived in the Yucatán Peninsula, trading had become a profession that Maya nobles controlled. They arranged marriages between their children to expand their trading empires. Maya merchants used jade, a green semiprecious stone for money. Artists and craftspeople sometimes traveled with the traders. They spread the Maya style of sculpture and mural painting to many parts of Mesoamerica.

AZTEC TRADERS

The people who lived in the Valley of Mexico first began trading manufactured goods in about A.D. 200. Workers of the city of Teotihuacán started workshops to produce more stone tools than they needed. They also organized pottery workshops that made jars and small figures. At first women in the Valley of Mexico shaped pottery with their hands for their own use. Then men began making pottery and using molds to shape the jars and figurines that they made in order to make more pottery more quickly. Other workshops made jewelry. Archaeologists believe that the people of Teotihuacán traded these items to farmers for food.

By the time of the Aztec (Mexica), who established an empire in about A.D. 1100, many of the people living in large cities made trade goods. The Aztec organized craftspeople into guilds. Guilds are professional associations that control the quality of work and set prices. The Aztec had at least 30 guilds. These included guilds for jewelers, goldsmiths, and feather workers. They also had guilds for salt makers and stonecutters.

In addition to organizing crafts guilds, the Aztec also created guilds of merchants and traders. Some of these professional traders, who were called *pochteca,* traveled thousands of miles in order to exchange goods with other groups of Indians who were not part of the Aztec empire. Because attacking an Aztec merchant was cause for war, they were assured safe passage throughout Mesoamerica. They carried weapons in case they were attacked. The largest and most powerful merchant guilds were located in the cities of Tenochtitlán and nearby Tlatelolco.

Aztec merchants carried gold dust, gold ornaments, knives that they made from flaked obsidian, and cotton clothing to trade. They exchanged these items for animal skins, jade, amber, and brightly colored feathers that Aztec craftspeople used in their work. They also traded for vanilla and chocolate.

In addition to trading for small items, Aztec merchants also traded for food. The people who lived in Tenochtitlán and the cities that surrounded it needed a constant supply of food. Using tlatmemes to carry food over long distances was not practical. Food was heavy to carry and it often spoiled if it was not eaten quickly. The Aztec grew most of their food outside the big cities in the Valley of Mexico and used shallow dugout canoes to transport it over lakes, rivers, and canals to markets in the cities.

△▽△▽△▽△▽△▽△▽△▽△▽△▽△▽△▽△▽△▽△▽

MOVING TRADE GOODS ACROSS MESOAMERICA

Porters, or burden carriers, called *tlatmemes* carried the goods that the merchants traded. They packed trade items on their backs in woven containers or tied to backpack frames that were covered with hides. The *tlatmemes* balanced and supported loads that weighed about 50 pounds by using a tumpline, a strap that crossed the forehead.

From the age of five years old, future tlatmemes were trained to use a tumpline. The Aztec burden carriers moved goods about 13 to 18 miles in a day. They were stationed in towns along the trade routes and often carried goods in relays instead of for the entire journey.

▽△▽△▽△▽△▽△▽△▽△▽△▽△▽△▽△▽△▽△▽

These people are using a pole to move a flat-bottomed boat down a canal in Mexico in 1884 or 1885. The ancient Aztec used boats and poles like the ones in this photo to supply food to the people who lived in the Aztec capital of Tenochtitlán. *(Library of Congress, Prints and Photographs Division [LC-USZ62-88753])*

Traders sold many of the goods that they had obtained at open-air markets. Sellers rented space and placed their wares on blankets spread on the ground. Every town in the Aztec Empire had a market. The town markets tended to specialize in what they sold. Some were noted for their painted gourds, and others for their dogs or clothing. Large cities had markets in each district, as well as a huge market held in the central civic plaza. Merchants made schedules so that nearby smaller markets were not held on the same day. The larger city markets often operated every day.

The largest market in the Aztec Empire was held in Tlatelolco. The conquistador Hernán Cortés wrote about this market, "There is one square twice as large as that of the city of Salamanca [a city in Spain], surrounded by arcades where there are daily assembled more than 60,000 souls, engaged in buying and selling." Each kind of merchandise was grouped into its own section. Everything was sold, from needles, thread, and rope, to building materials, clothing, and gold jewelry. Food vendors made tamales, meat wrapped in tortillas, and cooked stews and other dishes on stoves they set up in the marketplace. Other merchants sold groceries.

When people bought items at Aztec marketplaces, they paid with woven cotton capes and with bird feather quills that were filled with gold dust. They used cacao beans—the beans used to make chocolate—for smaller purchases and to make change. Sometimes copper axes were also used to pay for goods. Merchants added purchases on an abacus, a portable calculating device that was made from dried corn kernels. The kernels were threaded on string and moved up and down as a way to add and subtract that was faster than using one's memory.

The people of Mesoamerica continue to sell goods in outdoor marketplaces today as these Maya women are doing.
(© Philip Baird www.anthroarcheart.org)

The guardians of the marketplace, who belonged to the merchants' guild, supervised the marketplace. In addition to collecting fees from vendors, they made certain that the quality of the goods being sold was high. They also checked to see if the merchants were charging fair prices. Aztec merchants used handheld scales to weigh purchases. They measured the quantity of items such as corn in boxes that were made to standard sizes. If a merchant was caught cheating customers or shoppers were caught shoplifting he or she was brought before a judge and punished.

ANDEAN TRADERS

The Indian people of the Andes mountain region of South America began trading about 3,500 years ago. Researchers have found a trade route that they used at least 2,500 years before the Inca began

American Indians of Mesoamerica and South America traded woven cloth for other items that they wanted or needed. This Arcanian woman from Chile is weaving in the traditional way that Indian women wove for centuries. *(Archive of Hispanic Culture/Library of Congress, Prints and Photographs Division [LC-USZ62-75211])*

creating their empire in about A.D. 1000. This 150-mile-long route connected about 100 settlements. The people who lived there traded plant medicines, honey, hides, hardwood, and gold. The people of one village made pottery that they traded with other villages along this route. Today the trade route is a dirt road that leads from the mountains to the tropical rain forest and it is still used for trading.

The Chavin people obtained obsidian stones from 300 miles away from their main city, Chavin de Huántar, through trade. Chavin culture arose in fertile river valleys of what is now Peru in about 1000 B.C. The Chavin people also traded turquoise and quartz beads and objects made from sheets of gold.

Later, in about 100 B.C. the Nazca, whose culture arose in the southern part of what is now Peru, traded their pottery well to the north. They traded it for *Spondylus* shells that are obtained off the coast of Ecuador many miles to the north. These spiny shells were highly valued throughout South America.

Although the people who lived in and near the Andes had a long history of trading, when the Inca came to power they outlawed all exchanges of goods except on the borders of their empire. The Inca government had strict laws that controlled both trade and immigration. They obtained the goods that they needed by conquering new territory and ordering the people who lived there to work to produce goods for them. The Inca stored these items in warehouses throughout their empire. Government workers distributed them to the people so there was no need for markets in Inca cities.

American Indians of northern South America who had not been conquered by the Inca did continue to trade with one another. They exchanged precious stones, salt, gold, fish, and cloth.

ANCIENT ECUADORIAN TRADERS

In 1525 Spanish conquistadores reported that mysterious traders had visited the port of Zacatula in west Mexico. The traders stayed for several months before heading south by sea. For years their origins remained a mystery. Modern archaeologists think that they came from city-states or chiefdoms on the northwest coast of what is now Ecuador.

Clothing styles and styles of pottery indicate contact between the ancient cultures of northwestern Ecuador and western Mexico. Metalwork of Ecuador and of west Mexico was similar as well. Both

Ancient traders of what are now Ecuador and western Mexico used T-shaped or ax-shaped coins that were made from copper as a form of money.

cultures had formulas for making copper and arsenic alloys. They made many of the same types of metal objects as well. The metalwork in western Mexico arose suddenly, well after the South American metalworkers developed their techniques. The traders probably taught the people of Mexico how to work with metal. The two cultures first traded in about A.D. 600 to 700.

These merchant sailors of South America traveled over 2,400 miles of open sea in order to trade. They sailed on balsa wood rafts that had moveable centerboards and rigged sails. Spanish explorer Francisco Pizarro encountered one of these rafts as he voyaged across the northwest coast of South America in the 1500s. The raft was loaded with textiles that merchants were trading for *Spondylus* shells. Pizarro's men examined the goods and wrote of seeing brightly dyed llama and alpaca wool clothing that was embroidered with yarn.

AMAZON AND CIRCUM-CARIBBEAN TRADERS

Tribes of the Amazon basin traded weapons and curare, a poison that they used to coat the tips of their darts. Often they traded with people of the Circum-Caribbean. Arawak, Taino, and Carib Indians of the Circum-Caribbean traveled across the 1,700 miles of water between the Caribbean and northeast coast of South America to trade with people of the Amazon.

Circum-Caribbean merchants also traded with the Maya of Mesoamerica. They traded tobacco, weapons, tools, cloth, gold, and feathers, as well as conch shells and turtle shells. These traders also exchanged food between islands in the Caribbean, including dried fish and pineapples that they grew. The Indians of what is now Grand Turk Island made disk-shaped beads from shells. They traded these beads as luxury goods.

THE COMING OF THE SPANIARDS

At first the Spanish conquistadores traded with the Indians in order to obtain gold and information about where to find it. They also traded for samples of plants to take back to Spain. After conquest, the Spaniards did not need to trade.

When the conquistadores had removed the Indian leaders from power, they melted down their gold jewelry and sent gold bars back to Spain. They forced the Indians to mine for more gold and for silver as well. Historians believe that in 1492 about $200 million in gold and money existed in Europe. That amount tripled within 50 years. Most of this new wealth was taken from the Americas at the expense of the Indian people.

Spanish colonists took over the Indian salt making and textile weaving industries in the Yucatán. In the south, the Spaniards confiscated the Maya cacao plantations. The Indian people of the Mesoamerica, South America, and the Circum-Caribbean were forced to work as slaves and give everything they made or grew to the Spaniards.

TIME LINE	
1700 B.C.	Olmec traders begin trading rubber throughout Mesoamerica.
1500 B.C.	Indians of Peru establish a trade route through the Andes connecting 100 villages.
A.D. 200	The people of Teotihuacán begin manufacturing trade goods.
A.D. 600–A.D. 700	Traders of Ecuador travel 2,400 miles over the ocean to trade with the people of west Mexico.
A.D. 600–A.D. 900	Maya Traders of Mesoamerica travel long distances over the sea to trade.

Transportation on Water

American Indian people made boats so that they could travel over water to trade and to fish. The boats that they built were adapted to the rivers, lakes, or oceans where they lived. Indian boats were so well designed that Europeans who arrived in the Americas often copied the style of these boats. Two of these boat designs, the kayak and the canoe, are still used for outdoor recreation by many people today.

KAYAKS

Kayaks are lightweight boats. American Indians of the Arctic invented them for ocean travel. The Inuit made single-person kayaks from seal or walrus skin. They stretched the animal skin over a frame that they had made from wood and whalebone.

Usually men made the frames. First they bent wood or whalebone to make the gunwale, the framework around the top part of the boat. Then they drilled holes in the underside of this framework and fitted the ends of U-shaped crosspieces into them. To make sure that these pieces held, they fastened them with wooden nails.

Inuit women sewed the hides that covered the entire frame except for a small opening at the top where the person who paddled sat. They invented a special folded seam in order to keep the small vessels from leaking. After they finished, they covered the hides with seal oil to make them waterproof. Sometimes they attached a hooded parka to the cockpit of the kayak with waterproof seams. This kept paddlers (who were men) dry and warm.

American Indians living in the northern regions of North America made kayaks to travel over the ocean. Kayaking is a popular sport today. *(National Archives and Records Administration Pacific Alaska Region/Photograph No. NRIA-WME-PHOTOS-P899)*

The men, who used the kayaks for hunting seal and walrus, moved them through the water with a double paddle. They dipped first one end into the water and then the other. This increased their speed. In calm seas a man in a kayak could travel about 70 miles a day. The double paddle is a unique invention of the Inuit people of the Arctic and the native people of Siberia, the northernmost part of Asia.

The kayaker balanced the boat by sitting upright and leaning to shift his weight. When stormy seas caused the kayak to tip over, the man who paddled it could right it (turn it upright) with one arm. Because of their shape and the fact that they were light in weight, kayaks could be turned sharply. This took a great deal of practice to master. Young boys were given small kayaks when they were about 10 years old so that they could become experts at using them. By the time they were about 20 years old, they were expected to build their own kayaks.

For whale hunting and carrying cargo, the Inuit used boats called *umiaks*. These were larger than kayaks. They were from 20 to 30 feet long and five to six feet across. Unlike kayaks, umiaks had an open deck. Several people could ride in one. During whale hunts, the Inuit paddled these boats close to the whales and speared the sea mammals with harpoons, long spears with barbed points. Whale meat and blubber, or fat, was an important source of food for the Inuit people.

CANOES

Indians of North America, Mesoamerica, and South America made canoes for water travel. Canoes are slender boats that are paddled. The word *canoe* comes from *kenu,* a word the Taino people living in the Caribbean taught Christopher Columbus. The Taino used the word to mean a boat carved out of a tree. Later explorers used *canoe* to describe any American Indian boat.

Dugout Canoes

North American Indians who lived in the Northwest, California, the Circum-Caribbean, and the Southeast traveled in dugout canoes. They made a dugout by cutting down a large tree and splitting it in half. Then they scraped off the bark with shell scrapers and removed the tree branches with stone axes. To hollow out the inside of the boat, they often built a small fire on the flat side of the split log. Once the fire had burned down they could easily scrape away the charred wood to shape the boat.

The Nootka and Haida of the Northwest were expert boatbuilders. They made their canoes in many shapes and sizes. The largest of these canoes were made for ocean travel and could hold as many as 50 people. Indians of the Northwest used these large canoes to carry war parties. Canoes of the Northwest were sturdy and could quickly cover great distances over open water.

To make a dugout canoe, Indians of the Northwest first cut a large redwood or red cedar tree and trimmed off the bark and branches. They used redwood and red cedar trees because these trees grow to a huge size and their wood contains a resin that is resistant to water. Using stone chisels, wedges, and hammers, the boat makers shaped the log so that it was flat on the bottom. Then the builders worked to hollow out the inside of the boat. When a dugout of the Northwest was finished, the wood on the bottom of the boat was only about two inches thick. At the top of the boat the sides tapered to about three-quarters of an inch in thickness.

The next step of boatbuilding was to make the boat wider in the middle. Wider boats are less likely to tip over and could hold more people and cargo than if they were left in their original log shape. In order to make the wood easier to bend, Indians of the Northwest filled the half-finished canoe with water. Then they dropped red-hot stones that they had heated in a fire into the water. As the water boiled, the wood softened.

When the wood could be more easily bent, they wedged cross-pieces of wood into the opening to give the boat its desired shape. They also attached pieces of wood that they had carved to the back and front of the canoe to form the stern and bow. Finally they

Throughout the Americas, Indians made dugout canoes by setting fires atop large logs to make the wood in the center easier to remove. These people, who lived in what is now Virginia, used seashells to scrape away the charred wood. This engraving was made by Theodore de Bry in the late 1500s. *(Library of Congress, Prints and Photographs Division [LC-USZ62-52443])*

This traditional dugout canoe floats on the Trinity River on the Hoopa Reservation in California. *(National Archives and Records Administration Pacific Alaska Region/Photograph No. NRIS-75-PAOIRRIGATION-62[1])*

finished the opening by fastening strips of wood all the way around. The last step of boatbuilding was to decorate the boat by carving and painting it.

Birch-bark Canoes

Before the early 1500s American Indians of the Northeast traveled and fished in dugout canoes. Then they began building lightweight white cedar frames that they covered with birch bark or occasionally elm bark. Bark canoes could float in as little as four inches of water and were perfect for travel in shallow rivers and streams. Because a dry 15-foot canoe weighed only about 40 pounds, an Indian traveler could easily carry it past shallow stretches of stream or between rivers. Despite its weight, a relatively small canoe could hold a ton of cargo. Indians of the Northeast made canoes in many sizes, from single-person canoes all the way to large canoes that carried many people.

Indians of the Northeast began making a canoe by building the top part of the frame. They fastened two long pieces of wood together at the ends and wedged shorter crosspieces between them near the middle. When they had made the top of the canoe, they used it as a pattern and pounded stakes into the ground all the way around it.

Next they removed the stakes and laid them by the holes that they had made. They set the top of the canoe aside. Then they centered a

▲▼▲▼▲▼▲▼▲▼▲▼▲▼▲▼▲▼▲▼▲▼▲▼▲

HARVESTING BARK

Indians of the Northeast stripped bark from birch trees early in the summer by making a slit along the trunk. This allowed them to peel the bark away from the tree in a roll large enough to cover a canoe. To make the bark easier to work with, they soaked it in water to soften it.

▼▲▼▲▼▲▼▲▼▲▼▲▼▲▼▲▼▲▼▲▼▲▼▲▼

large piece of bark that they had stripped from a tree over the holes. The inside of the bark was more waterproof than the rough outer bark, so they faced it outward on the canoe. Then they set the frame back in place on top of the bark, matching it to the holes they had made. They used the frame as a pattern. After this the canoe builders placed heavy stones on the frame to make sure it did not move.

These Montagnais men are making the frame for a birch-bark canoe. The Montagnais live in Quebec, Canada. This picture was taken in 1863. *(Alexander Henderson/National Archives of Canada/Photograph No. PA-149709)*

When the canoe builders had positioned the frame over the bark, they made slits around the sides of the piece of bark. They left the bark that would serve as the bottom of the canoe uncut. Then they bent the bark to form the sides of the canoe. They held the sides in place by putting the sticks back into the holes that they had made in the ground earlier. After they had taken the stones from the canoe frame, the men pulled it up into position at the top of the canoe.

Next, women punched holes in the bark at the top of the canoe. Then they threaded roots through these holes and tied the bark to the wooden frame top of the canoe. Before they used the roots, the women soaked them in water to soften them. Then they split them so that this cord would be finer. When the women had finished this step they turned the canoe over.

American Indian women were responsible for waterproofing and repairing birch-bark canoes. Many Indian people used birch bark for their houses, such as the one in the background. This picture was taken in Ontario in 1872. *(National Archives of Canada/Photograph No. PA-074670)*

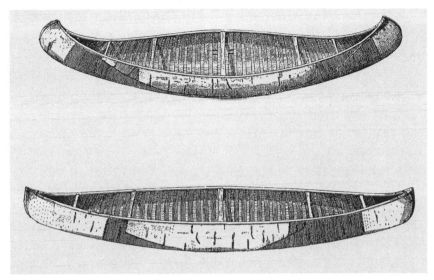

Birch-bark canoes weighed about 40 pounds and could be easily carried between rivers and streams. Europeans quickly began using this way of traveling. (U.S. Bureau of Ethnography)

They fixed any holes or tears on the bottom by sewing on bark patches. Then they sewed together the ends of the canoe. When they had finished, they turned the canoe over and covered the inside with pine or spruce pitch that they had heated. Pitch is the dried, sticky sap from trees. This coating of pitch made the canoe waterproof.

Men lined the inside of the canoe with very thin strips of wood. This lining made it strong. After the lining was in place, they steamed pieces of white cedar to soften them. Then they bent them into a bow shape and placed them crosswise into the canoe to form ribs. As they dried, the ribs pushed outward on the hull, making it rigid. Finally the canoe makers caulked the outside seams on the covering with hot pitch mixed with animal fat to seal them.

Europeans who came to the Northeast quickly adopted bark canoes. European fur traders depended on canoes to transport hides. The fur traders, who worked for large trading companies, followed the complex network of river routes that Indians had established. These routes allowed Indians to travel hundreds of miles using their canoes. People still use canoes for fishing and enjoyment today. Even though the materials that are used to make canoes have changed, the design of today's canoes is the same as that invented by the Indians of the Northeast.

NAVIGATORS OF MESOAMERICA

The Maya, who used dugout canoes for trading, routinely paddled their boats on the ocean. One popular route was between what is now the state of Campeche in the Yucatán Peninsula of Mexico to a port on the Rio Ulúa in what is now Honduras.

The Maya were experts at navigation. They studied wind patterns and water currents. When they traveled south, they kept close to the coastline and used the southern currents along the coast to help them row from port to port. On the return journey, they traveled farther away from the coast in order to take advantage of the Gulf Stream, a powerful ocean current that moves in a northerly direction. Modern historians, who have re-created the journeys of the Maya traders, estimate that they traveled about 30 miles a day.

Maya sailors made maps, but the coastline along which they traveled did not have many natural landmarks that were easy to notice. They met this challenge by creating their own landmarks. The Maya placed signals along the coastline so that sailors would always know where they were. Early European explorers wrote about several types of signals. They reported that the Maya lit bonfires along the coast that produced dark smoke and that they put signals in trees. According to the European explorers, the Maya also positioned people with flags along the coast to direct sailors.

In addition, the Maya built stone lighthouses on hills along the sea. One lighthouse was located in the ancient city of Tulum on the Yucatán Peninsula. It looked like a small pyramid and had niches built into it that faced the ocean. A fire built inside it warned sailors of a dangerous reef offshore. A reef is a ridge of sharp rocks. In addition to building lighthouses, the Maya also marked sandbars and channels where the water was so shallow that a boat could get stuck.

Shipping Canals

The Aztec who lived in the central Valley of Mexico used dugout canoes to move goods from town to town on a network of canals that Indian engineers had built. Tenochtitlán, the capital of the Aztec Empire, was built on an island in the middle of a large lake. Although the city was connected to the lakeshore by four roads, or causeways, moving goods on water was more efficient than using roads.

Smaller cities sprang up on other islands in the lake, and others grew along the lakeshore. Some of these lakeshore cities were centered around docks. There, dockworkers loaded ships with goods that had been carried there over land. They also unloaded goods from the canoes so that porters could carry them to merchants in far-off cities, where they would sell them.

▲▽▲▽▲▽▲▽▲▽▲▽▲▽▲▽▲▽▲▽▲▽▲▽▲

FEEDING THE CITY DWELLERS
More than 200,000 people lived in Tenochtitlán. Their food had to be brought to the island. Most of the cargo carried in canoes consisted of produce, corn, salt, and building materials.

▼▲▼▲▼▲▼▲▼▲▼▲▼▲▼▲▼▲▼▲▼▲▼▲▼

The Aztec created the shipping canals between *chinampas,* human-made islands on which they grew food crops and flowers. They began building the chinampas and canal system about 1,000 to 2,000 years ago. By the late 1500s, early Spanish colonists estimated that as many as 50,000 canoes carried goods over this canal system.

Aztec canoes ranged in length from 15 to 50 feet. Some of the canoes had only one or two people on them, while others carried as many as 60 people. The largest canoes carried more than eight tons of cargo. Archaeologists who have experimented to learn more about the canoes and canal system believe that one person could push a ton of goods along the canals using a pole. Aztec canoe polers often worked at night, when the temperature was cool, in order to keep the fruits and vegetables that they transported fresh.

American Indians of the southeastern part of North America also built canals. Researchers have found a system of two canals near Lake Okeechobee in what is now Florida. The Indians used shovels that they made from shells and wood to dig out millions of yards of sand and earth. The canals are seven miles long and were built in about A.D. 200. Indians used them to avoid a rapid in a river that ran from the lake to the Gulf of Mexico.

Rafts and Reed Boats

Traders from what is now Ecuador in the northern part of South America made oceangoing rafts, or flat-bottomed boats. These rafts were the largest floating vessels that American Indians made. To construct the rafts, the builders tied balsa wood logs together with ropes that they made from sturdy plant fibers. When they had finished the deck, they added a mast to hold a cotton sail. The sail caught the wind and powered the rafts across the ocean to Mesoamerica. In addition to space to tie cargo, the rafts had a shelter, as well as a

Single-person reed rafts were used by Indian people to fish along the coastline of what is now Peru. *(Library of Congress, Prints and Photographs Division [LC-USZ62-10634])*

▲▼▲▼▲▼▲▼▲▼▲▼▲▼▲▼▲▼▲▼▲▼▲▼▲▼▲▼

INFLATABLE RAFTS

The Inca invented inflatable rafts to ship heavy loads of guano. (Guano is bird droppings.) Inca workers gathered guano from islands off the coast of what is now Peru. Farmers used guano for fertilizer. To make sure their rafts did not sink beneath the weight of the guano, they filled sealskins with air, sealed them and attached them to the bottom of their rafts.

▼▲▼▲▼▲▼▲▼▲▼▲▼▲▼▲▼▲▼▲▼▲▼▲▼▲▼▲▼

hearth where sailors could cook their food. When they wanted to stay in one place, they dropped anchor. One way that archaeologists can tell where these sailors traveled is by finding the ring-shaped stone anchors that they used. Several have been found along the Mesoamerican coastline.

Balsa trees are native to the American tropical forest. The wood from these trees weighs only about six to nine pounds per cubic foot. Because it weighs so little, it floats easily. Modern boatbuilders laminate balsa wood with fiberglass to make hulls for speedboats and sailboats. In the 1950s surfers began constructing surfboards out of balsa wood. Although today most surfboards have foam cores, those made of balsa are still considered the best.

For centuries South American fishers used reed boats to travel up and down the west coast of what is now Peru. They navigated the ocean waters close to the coastline in one-person boats that were made from reeds. They also used them on large lakes.

The people of the coast picked the reeds when they had grown to their tallest height. After drying the reeds on the beach, they gathered them into long bundles. Then they tied the bundles together to shape the boat. Many of the reed boats that were used on the ocean had upward-curving points at the back and front. This allowed the boats to ride atop the waves much like surfboards. The fishers tied a stone to a rope and dropped it into the water when they wanted to anchor themselves in one place. They paddled the boats with a long piece of cane. When the Spanish conquistadores saw the boats, they called them *caballitos*, which means "little horses." People from some villages on the coast of Peru still fish from the reed boats today.

4

Transportation on Land

Water routes did not always lead to places where Indians needed to go, so they walked to many destinations. Traveling through deep snow presented challenges, especially when they had to carry loads. Indians of the Arctic, Subarctic, and Northeast invented snowshoes, toboggans, and sleds to make winter travel easier.

American Indians used the animals in their environment as helpers. The Inuit of the Arctic trained teams of dogs to pull sleds over snow and ice. Plains Indians used dogs to carry loads in packs and to pull loads. In the Andes of South America, Indians trained llamas to carry burdens on their backs.

When speed was important, Indian runners in many parts of the Americas carried messages from place to place. Horses had lived in the Americas in ancient times, but they became extinct about 11,000 years ago. After the Spanish conquistadores reintroduced horses to the Southwest in the 16th century, some Indian tribes of North

THE WHEEL

Although the Maya of Mesoamerica invented the wheel independently from people of other world cultures, they did not use the wheel for wagons or carts. No animals native to the Americas that could be domesticated were large enough to pull heavily loaded wagons.

America adopted horses for transportation. Runners remained important as message carriers even among these tribes because they were more difficult to detect than people on horseback. They could also travel routes that horses sometimes could not.

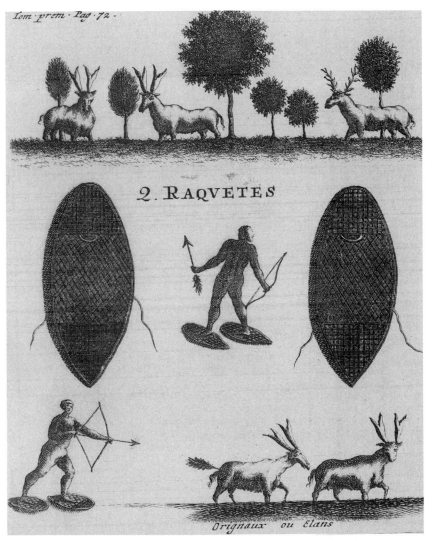

American Indians made snowshoes by lashing strips of rawhide and sinew (the fiber that holds animals' muscle to their bones) to wooden frames. This drawing of Indians hunting deer was made in 1703. Indians wore warm clothing in winter. European-American artists sometimes drew American Indians without clothing in order to make them appear to be uncivilized. *(Library of Congress, Prints and Photographs Division [LC-USZ62-115626])*

SNOWSHOES

Snowshoes were traditionally made from wooden frames that are laced with a netting of rawhide strips. (Today's high-tech snowshoes are more likely to be made of metal and plastic.) They distribute the wearer's weight over a large area so that he or she can walk on the surface of the snow. Indians from the Arctic Circle to the Great Lakes used snowshoes for winter travel. The Inuit of the Arctic also used them to cross sea ice.

Indians in the North American Northeast made snowshoes by bending a wooden frame into an oval with a point on one end. The point became the heel of the snowshoe. The Cree and other subarctic people made snowshoes by bending the rounded front of the frame upward and then lacing it with netting. Some tribes made snowshoes that were shorter and more rounded. The size of snowshoes that Indians made depended on the size of the person who would wear them.

American Indians fastened snowshoes onto their feet with leather straps. By lifting the toe of the snowshoes and dragging the heel as they walked, they made steady progress over deep snow that would otherwise be impassable.

TOBOGGANS

The Chippewa (Anishinabe) who lived near the Great Lakes invented the toboggan for winter travel. A toboggan is a long, narrow sled with a flat bottom and no runners. People or dogs pulled toboggans.

Toboggans allowed American Indians to move heavy loads over long distances. This drawing was made around 1856. Both the man and woman are wearing snowshoes. *(Cornelius Krieghoff/National Archives of Canada/Accession No. 1989-479-26)*

To make a toboggan, Indians heated hardwood by boiling it. This softened it enough so that they could bend the front of the sled into an upward curve. Indians tied loads to their toboggan with rawhide strips. They sometimes tied another strap to the back of the sled for a brake. A person would walk behind and pull on the strap to stop the toboggan if it went out of control.

Early French explorers used toboggans. Later non-Indian settlers in the Midwest also used them to travel where wagons were not practical. Today toboggans are used for winter recreation in many parts of the world.

> The word *toboggan* is a French mispronunciation of the Chippewa *nobugidaban*. This word is really a combination of two words meaning "flat" and "drag."

DOGSLEDS

When American Indians of the Arctic and parts of the Subarctic needed to travel over long distances or carry very heavy loads in the wintertime, they used dogsleds. Wood is scarce in the Arctic because it is too cold for trees to grow there. Indian sled builders used the resources in their environment to construct sleds.

Some carved the runners for the bottom of their sleds from whale jawbones. Other Inuit people cut and sewed strips of sealskin to make runners. They filled them with moss and earth. Then they poured water over them. When the water froze, the runners became hard. Inuit people sometimes covered fish with rawhide and froze them. The fish were part of the sled and could also be eaten in an emergency.

Many Inuit connected the runners of their sleds with shorter pieces of antler, bone, or wood using leather thongs. This arrangement looked like a ladder. When rough snow and ice twisted the runners out of parallel, the sled bent enough so that it did not break apart. The leather fastenings worked like shock absorbers.

In order to make sure the heavily loaded sled would glide over the snow, the Inuit covered the sled runners with pieces of ivory from walrus tusks or whale teeth. Sled drivers also melted snow in their mouths. When it melted, they rubbed the water over the runners. When it froze again the runners slid more easily over the snow.

The Indians of the Arctic trained teams of dogs to pull the sleds that were loaded with household goods or meat that they had hunted. Under good conditions a sled driver with a five-dog team could cover about 60 miles a day. A seven-dog team could pull a 900-pound load. The Inuit looked forward to the nine snowy months each year when they could quickly travel from place to place.

MALAMUTES

The ancestors of the Inuit domesticated, or tamed, a special kind of dog to pull their sleds. The dogs are called malamutes. They have thick, bushy coats. Some scientists believe that malamutes may have traveled with the Inuit on their journey from Siberia to what is now Alaska thousands of years ago. Others believe that Indian hunters domesticated North American wolves about 10,000 to 15,000 years ago. Malamute sled dogs are the closest relatives to wolves out of all dog breeds. Like wolves, sled dogs do not bark. They howl instead.

Because sled dogs were so important to the Inuit, they took very good care of them. In winter the Inuit built small snow houses for female malamutes carrying pups. They even made boots for their dogs' paws to protect them from ice crystals. Drivers started training puppies to pull sleds when they were two months old.

The Inuit of northern North America bred malamute dogs and trained them to pull sleds. *(Library of Congress, Prints and Photographs Division [LC-USZ62-92158])*

Indian people of northern North America used dogsleds to travel and carry goods from place to place. Arctic explorers and the U.S. government, which used sleds to carry mail, later borrowed this way of traveling. *(Canada Indian and Northern Affairs Collection/National Archives of Canada/Photograph No. PA-1006)*

Typically, men drove dogsleds. When the team was too slow, a woman might run ahead, pretending to cut meat to encourage the dogs to go faster. Often a driver would run ahead of his team to look for rocks or other hazards in the way. To keep from slipping when they ran or walked over the snow, the Indians of the Arctic attached bone or ivory grippers to the soles of their hide boots. Later they used double strips of sealskin to keep from slipping.

TRAVOIS

American Indians of the Great Plains used dogs to help them move their tipis and household items from camp to camp as they moved in search of game. Sometimes Indians tied a rawhide pack to a dog's back. Most of the time they made a small A-frame that they tied to the dog with leather straps.

To make the frame they laid two tipi poles on the ground and tied shorter sticks between them. Then they tied bundles onto this frame. Finally, they tied the ends of the poles to the dog's sides, so that the dog could drag the load behind. French explorers called this frame a *travois*. Because their dogs were quite small, Plains Indians needed to keep their tipis small. They could not collect many possessions.

The Spanish conquistadores brought horses with them to what is now New Mexico in the mid-1500s. Some of these horses ran away and became wild. Over the years, the size of the wild horse herds grew. The herds drifted northward. By the mid-1700s, Indians of the northern Plains began riding horses and using them to pull travois.

These Blood Indians from the Great Plains of Canada are using horses to pull their travois in this picture taken in 1910. Before horses, Plains Indians used dogs to pull travois. *(A. Rafton-Canning/National Archives of Canada/Photograph No. C-024277)*

This Indian woman is loading tipi poles onto a travois. Women were in charge of moving their homes. Because tipi poles and covers could be easily moved, Plains Indians could relocate entire villages. *(National Archives of Canada/Photograph No. PA-182256)*

Since a horse can pull loads that are 16 times heavier than a large dog can pull, Indians could carry more items when they moved.

TUMPLINES AND CRADLEBOARDS

American Indians invented two unique ways to carry burdens when they traveled on foot. The first invention was a tumpline. A tumpline is a strap or sling worn across the forehead. It supports and steadies a heavy object that is carried on the back. Indians of the Northeast used tumplines when they carried canoes between rivers. The people of Mesoamerica and South America also used tumplines to help them carry loads over both short and long distances.

Indians throughout the Americas used tumplines to carry heavy loads. Tumplines are unique to the Americas. *(After Felipe Guamán Poma de Ayala,* Nueva corónica y buen gobierno)

The second invention was the cradleboard, a frame with a soft pouch in which a baby is placed. Indians of North America and parts of South America used cradleboards to carry their babies when they traveled and when they worked. Cradleboards supported babies' heads and shaded their faces from the sun.

Indians of the Plains and the Southwest tribes used wood and leather to construct their carriers. California tribes wove their carriers like baskets. Inuit mothers carried their infants strapped on their backs beneath the parkas that they wore.

LLAMAS

Indians of the Andes Mountains of South America used llamas to carry loads. Llamas are members of the camel family. The people of

Indian mothers of the Plains and Northeast strapped their infants snugly into soft leather pouches before lacing them onto wooden-framed cradleboards. These pouches, called moss bags, were filled with dried moss to keep their babies dry and comfortable. *(Kansas State Historical Society, Topeka, Kansas)*

Llamas loaded with packs could easily manage the steep landscape of the Andes Mountains in South America. Indians of rural Peru still use llamas to transport goods today. *(Archive of Hispanic Culture/Library of Congress, Prints and Photographs Division [USH52-7176])*

the central Andes in what is now Peru began domesticating llamas between 6,000 and 7,000 years ago. At first they only herded the animals. By 3500 B.C., Indians had fully domesticated llamas and were breeding them as pack animals.

Llamas can carry loads of almost 90 pounds on long journeys and heavier loads on short ones. They travel at a rate of about 17 miles a day in high elevations and over rugged mountain terrain. Today people in the United States and Canada raise llamas to be used as pack animals for wilderness hiking (llama trekking).

RUNNERS

Throughout the Americas, specially trained Indian runners carried messages from one group of Indians to another. In the northeastern part of North America, the Iroquois had a system of runners in place along the 240-mile Iroquois trail that ran from near present-day Albany to Buffalo in what is now New York State. Many tribes that lived in the Southeast, the Plains, and the Great Lakes area also used runners.

Indian runners of California tribes trained daily and ate special diets. On long journeys they ate chia seeds, a high-energy nutritional source. Runners ate about a spoonful of chia seeds to run for many miles. The chia seeds that they ate are the same type of seeds that are sold today to grow "hair" or "fur" on pottery figurines. (The seeds sold in these kits have been treated with chemicals and should not be eaten. Some natural foods stores sell chia seeds that are safe to eat.)

CARRYING THE NEWS

Pueblo Indian runners of the Southwest played an important role in overthrowing the Spanish in 1680. A Pueblo Indian leader, Popé, told runners to spread word from pueblo to pueblo about a revolt that he had planned. He gave the runners hides with picture writing on them to carry. Popé also gave them knotted yucca cords. He told the runners to tell leaders of each pueblo to untie one knot each day. When they had untied all of the knots in these rope calendars, the revolt would begin. Runners traveled to at least 70 pueblos, some of them 300 miles away. Although the revolt was successful at driving out the Spaniards for a time, they returned later and defeated the Indians.

The Aztec of Mesoamerica also used runners. In 1519, when Spanish conquistador Hernán Cortés landed in what is now Mexico, Indians ran to tell the news to Montezuma (Moctezuma), the Aztec ruler. He was 250 miles away. According to Cortés, less than 24 hours passed before Montezuma knew that he and his men had landed.

The most organized system of runners was that of the Inca, who established an empire in South America in about A.D. 1000. (Indian people in the area had used runners for at least 500 years before the Inca organized them in the mid-1400s.) The Inca trained young men from the ruling class to run swiftly over short distances. Once they had finished training, the runners, who were called *chasqui*, lived in stone huts along the road system that the Inca built. The huts were spaced about two miles apart.

A blast on a conch shell horn warned a runner that another runner was approaching. The chasqui would leave the hut to meet the runner and receive the message. Some runners carried spoken messages that they had memorized. Others carried a quipu, a group of knotted colored strings that the Inca used to record information. Still other runners carried fabrics with messages coded into the designs.

Once the message had been passed, the waiting runner sped down the road to the next hut where yet another runner awaited. Relays of

Inca runners carried goods and information in relays. Using this system, as a team they could cover 150 to 300 miles a day. (*After Felipe Guamán Poma de Ayala, Nueva corónica y buen gobierno*)

runners could carry messages from 150 to about 300 miles a day using this system. It was so efficient that after conquest, the Spaniards continued to use it.

APPALOOSA HORSES

Indians of the North American Southwest, Plains, and Plateau began raising horses to ride as well as to pull burdens behind them on travois. By 1710 the Nez Perce of the Plateau region had began to breed horses. The Nez Perce liked spotted horses better than others. To raise the kind of horses they wanted, they mated the fastest and smartest spotted stallions (male horses) and mares (females) to produce the appaloosa horse. Appaloosa horses always have spots, and many have a light gray coat that is dappled with darker gray spots.

By 1858 the U.S. government had confined the Nez Perce to a 10,000-square-mile reservation. Ten years later the government reduced the size of the reservation to 1,000 square miles. In 1877 the U.S. government ordered the Nez Perce to move to the Lapwai Reservation in Idaho. Reluctantly the chiefs agreed. On the tribe's way to the new location, four white men were killed. The U.S. Army blamed the entire tribe. They wanted to attack all the Indians instead of punishing the individuals who were responsible for the deaths.

Under the leadership of Chief Joseph, the Nez Perce rode their appaloosa horses away from the soldiers. Through the Bitterroot Mountains and across Montana they evaded the soldiers for more than 1,000 miles.

HOW APPALOOSA HORSES WERE NAMED

For many years the Nez Perce maintained friendly relationships with early white settlers to the Wallowa Valley of what is now Oregon, where they lived. Those pioneers, as well, recognized the superiority of the Nez Perce horses. They called the animals *Palouse* after the river where the tribe grazed many of their horses. In time "a palouse horse" became shortened to *appalousey* and then *appaloosa*, the name that is used today.

The Nez Perce of the Plateau Region developed the appaloosa horse breed. This photograph of young men on appaloosa horses was taken in southeastern Idaho in 1879. *(National Archives and Records Administration of College Park/Photograph No. NWDNS-75-SEI-107)*

Not far from the Canadian border, the U.S. Army finally stopped them. Chief Joseph knew that his people were too weak to fight or escape, so he surrendered.

The U.S. Army took most of the tribe's appaloosa horses and sold them to local ranchers. Soldiers hunted down the horses that they could not capture and shot them. The army rewarded the soldiers with one bottle of whiskey for each Indian horse they killed. Over the next 50 years the breed almost became extinct.

In 1938 a group of horse lovers formed the Appaloosa Horse Club to preserve the breed and to make its history known. Members of the Nez Perce Tribe are also working to reconnect their people with the breed of horse that they created. In 1991 the Chief Joseph Foundation was established on the Nez Perce reservation to promote cultural pride and community healing through activities centering on the horses.

5

Trails, Roads, and Bridges

Indians of the Americas created a network of routes from place to place. They were such expert trail and road builders that many modern highways follow the routes that they laid out hundreds of years ago. The people of the Southwest, Mesoamerica, and the Andes Mountains in South America built formal road systems. Indians also built bridges to cross rivers and streams.

TRAILS

North American Indians cleared and maintained a large system of trails. Most of these trails were two to three feet wide. They marked these trails so that they were easy to follow. Two ways of marking trails were making piles of stones that would not occur in nature (called cairns) and cutting signs into tree trunks. Indians also bent branches of young trees and tied them in place with strips of sinew to show where trails were. Sinew is the tough fiber that holds animals' muscles to their bones. Tying the trees caused them to grow in an unnatural shape. Seeing such a tree would alert travelers that they were on a trail.

The Iroquois trail network in the Northeast ran from Canada to the Carolinas. American Indians created the Iroquois trail in the Mohawk Valley of upstate New York. (It is now U.S. Highway 40.) They established the Old Connecticut Path, which ran between what are now Albany, New York, and Boston, Massachusetts. Some other well-known Indian trails are the Old Sauk Trail, the Susquehanna Trail, and the Natchez Trace, which ran from Tennessee to Mississippi. Colonists traveling to what is now Kentucky renamed an Indian trail, the Warriors Path, naming it the Wilderness Road. Although the frontiersman Daniel Boone is sometimes credited with blazing this trail, he did not discover it. He widened an Indian trail.

Eventually the trails that Indians had created became pioneer wagon routes. The famous Santa Fe Trail, a route that connected the cities of St. Louis, Missouri, and Santa Fe, New Mexico, was built on an original Indian trail that extended from the Mississippi River to the northern part of Mexico. The 2,000-mile Oregon Trail that non-Indian settlers began using to travel from Council Bluffs, Iowa, to the Pacific coast had been established and used by Indians hundreds of years before.

▲▽▲▽▲▽▲▽▲▽▲▽▲▽▲▽▲▽▲▽▲▽▲▽▲▽▲▽▲▽▲

CITY SITES AND INDIAN TRAILS

Why did the American Indians build a trail between Albany and Boston before those cities were founded? They cleared land and built their own villages on sites that were near water and could be easily defended from attack. The trails that they created connected these villages. European colonists often established their own towns on the sites of Indian villages after removing the Indians. Not only were the sites well located, but the European colonists could begin building and farming immediately because they had already been cleared of trees.

At the time of European contact about 3,000 Massachuset Indians, a farming tribe, lived where Boston would be built. Albany, New York; Council Bluffs, Iowa; Kansas City, Missouri; and Detroit, Michigan, were all originally North American Indian settlements, as was the site of New York City.

North American colonists also located cities on established Indian trail routes. Chicago, Illinois, was founded on an Indian portage route between Lake Michigan and the Illinois River. City streets were also laid over Indian trails. Hennepin Avenue in Minneapolis, Minnesota, and Main Street in Los Angeles, California, were once Indian trails.

▽▲▽▲▽▲▽▲▽▲▽▲▽▲▽▲▽▲▽▲▽▲▽▲▽▲▽▲▽▲▽

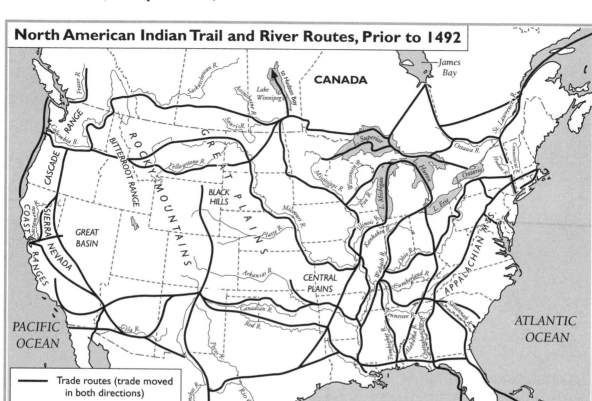

North American Indian Trail and River Routes, Prior to 1492

Cherokee/Scottish fur trader Jesse Chisholm established a trail used by cowboys to drive herds from Texas to the Kansas railheads. Chisholm created it as a wagon road in 1832 to haul freight from Kansas in order to stock his trading posts. Some historians credit him with being the father of the first chain of convenience stores because his posts sold provisions to the cattlemen on their way north. U.S. Highway 81 follows the route today.

Portage routes were short trails that linked rivers and lakes. Often boats would be carried over them from one body of water to the other. In the Northeast these portage routes connected rivers and lakes from the Hudson Bay to the Gulf of Mexico. A major river and portage route linked what would become Montreal, Quebec, and the Mackinaw Straits in the Upper Peninsula of what is now Michigan.

A route called the Grand Portage Route connected Lake Superior to what is now the Minnesota/Manitoba border. An offshoot of this route led to the Mississippi River.

ROADS

Roads are wider than trails. Their surface is often paved with stones or other materials. In North America, the Anasazi of the Southwest who lived in Chaco Canyon built roads to connect small outlying villages to a larger pueblo. The Hopewell people who lived in the Mississippi valley built a 60-mile road that connected two of the huge mounds that they built from earth. The Maya and Aztec people of Mesoamerica built some roads that were paved as well. The largest road system in the Americas was that of the Inca, who established an empire in about A.D. 1000 in what is now Peru. The Inca made many of their roads over old trails that had been made by other Indian people before them.

Ancient Roads of North America

In the southwestern desert, Anasazi road builders constructed 500 miles of curbed roadways that connected 75 communities in Chaco Canyon in what is now New Mexico. Anasazi culture arose in about 350 B.C. and flourished until about A.D. 1450. The longest road in the Chaco Canyon system is 42 miles long. The roads are straight and radiate from the canyon like spokes on a wheel. They were built in the 11th and 12th centuries.

Some Anasazi roads were about 30 feet across. To make them, builders leveled the earth and used rocks to build up low spots. They also lined the sides of the roads with rocks. The roads on steep slopes are narrow. There road builders carved stone steps or built earth ramps.

Some historians think that the high points along Anasazi roads may have been signaling stations. Recent research indicates that the roads may have served a religious purpose. Roads also helped to form many small communities into a single unit.

American Indians who lived in the Northeast and Southeast made trails instead of roads. One exception is a straight, 60-mile-long road between two Hopewell villages. These villages are now the sites of the towns of Newark, Ohio, and Chillicothe, Ohio. The Hopewell lived in the river valleys in the lower Midwest from about 100 B.C. to A.D. 400.

Ancient Roads of Mesoamerica

The Olmec, whose culture flourished between 1700 B.C. and 400 B.C., built trails and roads that became the foundation for the Maya road system. Maya culture arose in Mesoamerica in about 1500 B.C. Eventually Maya roads crisscrossed the Yucatán Peninsula. The longest known road in the Maya system was 60 miles long.

Maya roads were 13 to 20 feet wide. To construct them, builders made low stone retaining walls. They filled the space between them with large, flat stones. Then they covered these slabs with gravel. Archaeologists, who study the past, have found a large stone cylinder that the Maya may have used as a roller to smooth the roads. The builders surfaced many of their roads with cement that they made from burned limestone and wood ash. Because Maya roads were raised above the land, water drained from them. This was important in the rainy climate where the roads were located.

The Maya called their white limestone roads *sacbe*, which means "white road" in the Maya language. It also means "milky way." The Maya told conquistadores that the roads were sacred routes used for traveling to sacred places.

The Aztec, who established an empire in what is now Mexico in about A.D. 1100, built a roadway network in the Valley of Mexico. This network served to connect, their main city, Tenochtitlán, to surrounding communities. They made most of their roads from packed earth.

Tlatmemes, or porters, carried trade goods to and from Tenochtitlán, the Aztec capital, over four major roads. These 23-foot-wide causeways were built so that their surface was above the water in the lake that surrounded the city. This picture is based on one found in *Historia general de las cosas de Nuevo España* by Bernardo Sahagún. *(Library of Congress, RareBooks Division)*

Ancient Roads of South America

The Inca road system had two main, parallel roads that ran north and south. One was in the highlands, and the other ran along the Pacific coast from what is now northern Ecuador to southern Chile. A number of smaller roads connected villages. Inca builders used the same building methods for all of the roads that they made. Historians believe that engineers planned the roads and supervised their construction.

The roads that the Inca built varied in width from 82 feet to very narrow. The narrow parts of the road were carved into solid rock and zigzagged up mountain slopes. When the land made it necessary,

Inca engineers carved tunnels through hills. They lined some of these tunnels with stone. On flat ground they packed the earth and then surfaced it with gravel and cement. They also built long elevated roads called causeways over marshes and shallow streams.

▲▼▲▼▲▼▲▼▲▼▲▼▲▼▲▼▲▼▲▼▲▼▲▼▲▼▲

THE LONGEST ROADS

The Inca made the longest road system at the time in the world. It was at least 140,000 miles long, making it larger than the Roman Empire's road system, which was about 56,000 miles long. Roman roads were still used in Europe when the Inca built their roads.

▼▲▼▲▼▲▼▲▼▲▼▲▼▲▼▲▼▲▼▲▼▲▼▲▼▲▼

Where streams and rivers crossed the roadway, the Inca built bridges. They used ferryboats to cross very wide rivers.

In desert areas, Inca road builders sank posts into the ground to mark the road. Often they bordered roads with short walls to keep out drifting sand. Roads that ran through cities had stone walls on each side too. Where they could, the Inca planted shade trees beside their roads and constructed small aqueducts to water them. Every four and one-half miles, they placed distance markers so travelers would know how far they had journeyed. Rest houses for runners and barracks for soldiers were spaced along the road, as were storehouses for food, clothing, and weapons.

When Spanish conquistadores under the command of Francisco Pizarro began to overthrow the Inca Empire in 1531, they helped themselves to the food and supplies in the storehouses. The roads

▲▼▲▼▲▼▲▼▲▼▲▼▲▼▲▼▲▼▲▼▲▼▲▼▲

A SPANIARD'S ACCOUNT

The Spaniards were impressed by the Inca roads when, led by the conquistador Francisco Pizarro, they arrived in what is now Peru. Cieza de León, who traveled with Pizarro, wrote:

I believe there is no account of a road as great as this, running through deep valleys, high mountains, banks of snow, torrents of water, living rock, and wild rivers. . . . Oh! can anything similar be claimed for . . . any of the powerful kings who ruled the world that they were able to build such a road or provide the supplies found on it.

▼▲▼▲▼▲▼▲▼▲▼▲▼▲▼▲▼▲▼▲▼▲▼▲▼

Bridges were an important part of the Inca road system. Many bridges that they built were more complex than the one in this copy of a drawing by Felipe Guamán Poma de Ayala, an Indian historian and artist who lived in Peru in the early 1600s. (Nueva corónica y buen gobierno)

guided them throughout the empire and allowed them to move quickly forward in their campaign to claim the empire for Spain.

BRIDGES

In South America the Inca built bridges over streams and rivers. North American Indians of the Northwest built fishing bridges over rivers. Indians of the Southeast built bridges as well.

Inca Bridges

Some Inca bridges were simple, such as a log or stone slabs placed across a river and set onto piers. The Inca made other bridges by stringing a thick hemp rope across a river and fastening either end to sturdy trees or large boulders. They placed goods and people in a large basket with a thick wooden handle that hung on the rope. Then they slid the basket across the river.

Sometimes the Inca created floating pontoon bridges over calm water. They made them by braiding reeds over a hemp frame that they tied to balsa wood floats. Inca bridge builders built floating bridges in sections and tied them together with thick rope.

TOLL BRIDGES

The Inca road system contained more than 40 large suspension bridges and more than 100 small ones. Some of the larger ones spanned rivers that were about 150 feet wide. Bridges were so important to the Inca that they established laws that set punishments for anyone who tampered with one.

The Inca government charged tolls for crossing bridges. People who lived near the bridges maintained them. Workers changed the ropes every two years.

The Inca began building suspension bridges in the 1300s. They were hung on fiber ropes that often were as thick as a person's body. Builders used llama leather to strengthen the ropes. Inca workers buried the ends of the ropes about 20 feet beneath the surface of the ground on each side of the river. They anchored the ends with heavy wooden beams.

To erect the bridge, workers raised the ropes over wooden pillars on each side of the river close to the water. They made the walkway by tying ropes between the bases of the pillars and covering them with wooden boards. Suspension bridges were narrow, but they were very sturdy.

Conquistadores wrote letters home detailing their fear of crossing Inca suspension bridges because they swayed in the wind. (Suspension bridges were not built in Europe until 1810.) They overcame their fear and crossed bridges as they marched to Cuzco, the Inca capital, in 1533. After the Spaniards overthrew the Inca Empire, they continued to use many of the bridges until the 1800s. One bridge that was built in 1400 became known as the Bridge of San Luis Rey. It was used until 1880.

North American Indian Bridges

American Indians of the Northwest made bridges from wood. They used them for fishing. Each year when the salmon left the ocean and swam upstream to spawn, Indian fishers would stand on the bridges that they had made and spear salmon. They could spear more fish from a bridge than they could when they were standing on the riverbank.

Indians throughout the Southeast constructed wooden bridges that spanned rivers. These ranged from simple and fragile bridges to those that were much sturdier. When the Spaniard Hernando de Soto and his company explored the area between 1539 and 1543, they saw several bridges that Indians had built.

Three of de Soto's officers kept journals of their travels. They wrote about seeing an Indian bridge near the coast of Florida. Another Spanish explorer, Álvar Núñez Cabeza de Vaca, had crossed this same bridge a little less than 10 years earlier. De Soto and his men were unable to cross this bridge because they had brought horses and cattle. Since Indians had neither horses nor cattle, they did not build their bridges to hold these heavy animals.

The Spaniards also saw bridges in what is now Tennessee. One of de Soto's officers wrote, "They had bridges over the river made of wood, but so shaky and ruinous that they could hardly pass over them." These bridges were very near to an Indian stockade that housed a number of warriors. Probably these bridges were made so that they could be easily destroyed as a way to defend the village. Later, in what is now Indiana, de Soto's officer wrote, ". . . [W]e crossed a swamp in which the Indians had made a well-made bridge, broad and of ingenious construction."

Indians built this fishing bridge over the Wotsonqua River in British Columbia, Canada. Bridges like this one enabled Indians to catch more fish than they could by standing on riverbanks. This picture was taken in 1872. *(Charles Horetzky/National Archives of Canada/PA-009133)*

American Indians who lived in the southeastern part of North America built bridges. Spanish explorer Hernando de Soto encountered several in his travels and wrote about them. *(Library of Congress, Prints and Photographs Division [LC-USZ62-104375])*

MAPS AND GUIDES

American Indians were the first people to create maps of the Americas. Mostly they passed their knowledge of the landscape, trade routes, and villages by word of mouth. Sometimes they drew maps on hides, on birch bark, or on the ground. These maps were not preserved. Archaeologists believe that some rock drawings, or petroglyphs, may have represented hunting territories. Because American Indians relied on

▽▲▽▲▽▲▽▲▽▲▽▲▽▲▽▲▽▲▽▲▽▲▽▲▽▲▽▲▽▲

AZTEC MAPS

The Codex Mendoza, one of four surviving pre-Columbian manuscripts from Mesoamerica, contains maps that the Aztec used to show the land holdings of different families.

▽▲▽▲▽▲▽▲▽▲▽▲▽▲▽▲▽▲▽▲▽▲▽▲▽▲▽▲▽▲▽

This Indian guide, sitting at the summit of Groundhog Mountain, British Columbia, Canada, in 1899, helped engineers plan the route of a railroad to the Yukon Territory. American Indians had an extensive knowledge of geography. *(National Archives of Canada/PA-083049)*

their memories and did not always draw maps, early European American explorers took along Indian people to serve as guides. Sometimes they captured them for this purpose. Often Indian guides served as translators.

The first Indian mapmaker in historic times was a young man the Spaniards called Miguel. He was captured in 1601 by a group of explorers traveling through what are now Texas, Oklahoma, and Kansas. Don Juan de Oñate headed the party. The conquistadores took Miguel to Mexico City and asked him to draw a map of his homeland. Miguel noted the American Indian villages he had actually visited and then he drew a large area of the south-central plains that he had only heard about from others. Later his map was found to be very accurate.

Two hundred years later a Blackfeet chief named Ac ko mok ki drew a map on birch bark for a Hudson's Bay Company fur trader. The trader, who had stopped in what is now Alberta, Canada, wanted to know what lay ahead of him. Ac ko mok ki first told the trader and then began drawing a map in the snow. His map started where the men were standing and expanded to cover mountains and rivers within a 200,000-square-mile region all the way to what is now Wyoming. Ac ko mok ki's map included tribal groups, as well as their names and estimated populations. The trader copied the map on paper. Meriwether Lewis and William Clark relied on the information contained in this map three years later as they sought the Northwest Passage.

Sports and Games

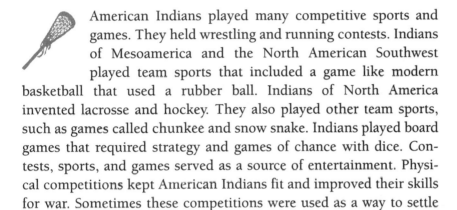

6

American Indians played many competitive sports and games. They held wrestling and running contests. Indians of Mesoamerica and the North American Southwest played team sports that included a game like modern basketball that used a rubber ball. Indians of North America invented lacrosse and hockey. They also played other team sports, such as games called chunkee and snow snake. Indians played board games that required strategy and games of chance with dice. Contests, sports, and games served as a source of entertainment. Physical competitions kept American Indians fit and improved their skills for war. Sometimes these competitions were used as a way to settle arguments.

BASKETBALL

About 3,000 years ago American Indians began playing a form of basketball. The Olmec, who lived in what is now Mexico from about 1700 B.C. to 400 B.C. invented the game. They used latex from the rubber trees that grew where they lived to make rubber balls. The Olmec built huge stone ball courts in the center of their cities. Eight-and-a-half-foot-tall stone walls surrounded the courts. Stone disks with holes in the center were mounted on the side walls. Players threw a rubber ball through the hole in the stone to make a goal. Mesoamerican ball players used both solid and hollow rubber balls to play their games.

From the Olmec, the game spread to the Maya and Aztec of Mesoamerica. (Maya culture arose in the lowlands of what is now Mexico in about 1500 B.C. The Aztec (Mexica) moved to the Valley of Mexico in about A.D. 1100.) Six hundred ball courts have been

Ancient basketball courts similar to this one at Xochlcalco, in Mexico, have been found throughout Mesoamerica and the Southwest. Players earned points by passing a rubber ball through vertical stone rings on the walls at each end of the court. *(Abbye A. Gorin Collection from the Latin American Library Photographic Archive, Tulane University)*

found in Mexico alone. Indians of the Southwest also played basketball. About 200 Hohokam ball courts have been found in what is now Arizona. The Hohokam culture arose there in about 300 B.C.

The basketball courts were built in two shapes. One was shaped like a capital T and the other a capital I. Courts were usually from 20 to 30 feet wide and 40 to 50 feet long, but some were much larger. A line on the ground divided the ball court in half.

Tiered stone seats built into the walls show that the games attracted large crowds. Ancient basketball courts also had special areas where the teams prepared and dressed for the game. The basketball players of Mesoamerica wore helmets when they played. Players also wore protective padding that included gloves, a broad waist belt, knee and hip pads, and special footwear. The sports helmet and protective clothing were woven from fiber, like baskets. Some were leather.

Archaeologists believe that there may have been two versions of the game. The first was a form of handball that used a small, solid rubber ball. Players could touch the ball in this game with their hands. The other game used a big rubber ball. Players had to move the ball from one end of the court to the other without using their hands. This game was played as a ceremony.

James Naismith, a gym teacher in Massachusetts, reinvented basketball in the United States. In winter 1891, he tried to modify the rules of lacrosse so that it could be played indoors. (Lacrosse was an American Indian game.) When that did not work, he made up a game in which players scored points by tossing the ball into peach baskets with the bottoms cut out. The baskets were mounted on the end walls of the gym. The modern game of basketball borrowed some of its defensive and offensive moves from lacrosse.

LACROSSE

American Indians who lived in many parts of North America played lacrosse. Sometimes called the fastest game on two feet, lacrosse is played by two teams on an open field with goals at each end. In the modern version of the game, there are 10 players on each team. Each player carries a stick with a mesh pocket at the end. Players try to put

▲▽▲▽▲▽▲▽▲▽▲▽▲▽▲▽▲▽▲▽▲▽▲▽▲▽▲▽▲▽▲

BASKETBALL AND THE CONQUISTADORES

Early Spanish conquistadores watched the Aztec play a basketball game that they called *tlachitli*. They admired the way the sport was played and commented on how skilled the players were. Hernán Cortés was so taken with the game that he took two teams back to Spain to play exhibition matches before European audiences. Basketball never caught on in Europe. In Mesoamerica the Catholic Church later banned all "heathenish practices" of the indigenous people, including the game of basketball.

▽▲▽▲▽▲▽▲▽▲▽▲▽▲▽▲▽▲▽▲▽▲▽▲▽▲▽▲▽▲▽

▲▽▲▽▲▽▲▽▲▽▲▽▲▽▲▽▲▽▲▽▲▽▲▽▲▽▲▽▲▽

WOMEN'S LACROSSE

Mainly young men played lacrosse, but some tribes allowed women to play on teams with men. In a few instances all-women teams competed with other women.

▼▲▼▲▼▲▼▲▼▲▼▲▼▲▼▲▼▲▼▲▼▲▼▲▼▲▼▲▼

a small, hard rubber ball into the opponents' net. They may not touch the ball with their hands.

North American Indians had many variations of the game. It was a dangerous one and required players to have great skill. Among the Cherokee and other Southeast tribes, the players often used two sticks to toss, catch, and pass a soft deerskin ball. Teams were composed of 100 to 1,000 players on each side. They were so

North American Indian lacrosse players used the game to train for war and to settle disputes without having to go to war. Players from various tribes made and used different styles of lacrosse sticks. This image of lacrosse players was drawn by George Catlin and was published in 1844. *(National Archives of Canada/Accession No. 1989-292-21)*

Unlike the modern version of lacrosse, the original game could be played by hundreds of players on a field that might be many miles long. This drawing by George Catlin shows the goalposts that were used. *(National Archives of Canada/Accession No. 1960-50-2.23)*

large that many players never got near the ball. These players used their netted sticks to injure other players in order to take them out of the game. The goals were located from 500 yards to half a mile apart. Sometimes they were several miles from each other. Some tribes erected goal posts and threw the ball between them to score points. Lacrosse games were played from dawn to sunset and lasted two to three days. The Cherokee called lacrosse "War's Little Brother."

Tribes, including the Chippewa (Anishinabe), Ho-Chunk, and Santee Dakota Sioux, played a version of the game that is called Great Lakes Lacrosse. These players used a three-foot stick with a small pocket and a wooden ball that was shaped into a sphere by charring the wood.

The Six Nations of the Iroquois, who live in southern Canada and parts of what is now New England and New York, called their version of the game *baggataway* or *twearaathon.* The Onondaga named it *dehuntshigwa'es,* which means "Men Hit a Rounded Object." Iroquois players used a stick longer than three feet that ended in a large, triangular pocket. Lacrosse sticks used in today's game are modeled after them. Iroquois players had a reputation for good sportsmanship and fair play. During harvest season, a time when Iroquois men did not hunt, lacrosse contests were held nearly every day.

French settlers in Canada were the first non-Indians to adopt the Indian sport. By the early 1800s they had begun to limit the number of players on each team and set measurements for a standard field. When the Dominion of Canada was formed in 1867, lacrosse was designated the country's national sport. Montreal's Olympic Club

Members of the lacrosse team of the Mohawk Nation at Caughnawaga in Quebec, Canada, were the Canadian lacrosse champions in 1869. By this time lacrosse had become a sport with rules resembling the game played today. *(James Inglis/National Archives of Canada/Photograph No. C-0011959)*

organized a team in 1844 to play against an Indian team. Other matches with Indian teams were held in 1848 and 1851. In 1856 the new Montreal Lacrosse Club made the first set of written rules for the game.

At the same time that others were learning to play and love the game of lacrosse, by the mid-1800s, many Indians in the northern United States had stopped playing the sport. Often they turned away from the tradition at the direction of government officials and missionaries who objected to the gambling that surrounded lacrosse games and believed that, because it was traditional, lacrosse would prevent Indian people from becoming "civilized." At the same time, non-Indian interest in lacrosse spread to the United States, where by 1870, several New York City teams were started. Colleges began forming teams too.

In 1867 a team of Indians traveled to England to play a match before Queen Victoria. Later non-Native Canadian and Iroquois teams toured Europe putting on matches. Eventually Indians began returning to the game that had traditionally been theirs. The Onondaga tribe started a team, and Glen "Pop" Warner, a football coach at the Carlisle Indian School in Pennsylvania, substituted lacrosse for baseball at the boarding school. "Lacrosse is a developer of health and strength," he said. "It is a game that spectators rave over once they understand it."

Today lacrosse has attracted more than half a million players in the United States. More than 250 colleges and 600 high schools have teams. More than 100 colleges and universities and 150 high schools have women's teams. The Iroquois Lacrosse Association preserves the traditional game among the tribes that made up the Iroquois Confederacy.

HOCKEY AND OTHER TEAM SPORTS

Both field hockey and ice hockey are based on an American Indian stickball game that was called shinny. Tribes throughout North America played it. The players used a wooden ball or one made of buckskin. They could only touch it with a stick or kick it with their feet. Indians often played shinny on ice.

The name *hockey* came from the Jesuit missionaries who watched Indians living in what is now Canada playing the game. *Hoquet* is the French word for a shepherd's crook. The missionaries used it to refer to the curved sticks the players used to propel the ball down the playing field.

MORE GAMES OF SKILL

American Indians played a number of games that required skill and coordination. In the winter Indians of the Northeast played a game known as snow snake. They made a track by pressing a log into snow so that it made a depression. Then they packed the snow so that the surface would be more slippery. Most snow snake tracks were a quarter of a mile to a mile long.

The equipment for snow snake consisted of carved sticks that were between three feet and six feet long. These sticks were rounded at the top and flat on the bottom. Snow snake players decorated their sticks to look like snakes. They shaped and polished the sticks so that they would travel far over the snow.

To play the game, each player took a turn running toward the track

▲▽▲▽▲▽▲▽▲▽▲▽▲▽▲▽▲▽▲▽▲▽▲▽▲▽▲

BOWLING
Archaeologists have found a number of stone balls in places where ancient Indians lived in what are now Georgia and Alabama. At a mound site in Georgia they found two alleyways built of stone and hard clay. Some believe that Indians used these alleys and stone balls to play a game similar to bowling.

▽▲▽▲▽▲▽▲▽▲▽▲▽▲▽▲▽▲▽▲▽▲▽▲▽▲▽

and releasing a wooden snake so that it slid down the track. The player whose snake traveled the farthest without jumping out of the track was the winner. Skilled players were known to propel their snakes over a mile through the snow.

Indians of the Southeast played a game called chunkee. (Sometimes it is spelled chunky, chunkey, or tchung kee.) They built their villages around a central courtyard where they played the game. To play chunkee, Indians held long poles or lances. They would all stand at one end of the field and at a signal they would begin

Indians of the Americas played a number of games that kept them fit as well as provided a way to have fun. This engraving by Theodore de Bry was first published in the late 1500s. *(Library of Congress, Prints and Photographs Division [LC-USZ62-068528])*

△▽△▽△▽△▽△▽△▽△▽△▽△▽△▽△▽△▽△▽

MARBLES

American Indian children played games with marbles. They used round stones and made the marbles from pitch, the sticky sap that hardens on fir trees. They also made marbles from clay.

▽△▽△▽△▽△▽△▽△▽△▽△▽△▽△▽△▽△▽

running. One of the players would roll a stone disk with a large hole in the center in front of them. The players threw their lances where they thought the stone would stop rolling. The person with the most accurate guess and aim won. In some versions of the game, they tried to spear the hole in the stone while it was in motion.

Tribes of the Great Plains played similar games using a hoop made from wicker or wood. Players sometimes tried to shoot an arrow or throw a spear into the center of the hoop. In other versions of this game, they tried to catch the hoop with long sticks as it rolled.

Women of the Plains played a foot bag game similar to those that people play today. They used balls that were about six to seven inches in diameter. These were stuffed with deer, antelope, or buffalo hair. The Cheyenne and Mandan of the Plains sometimes decorated the buckskin covers with elaborate porcupine quillwork.

Arapaho, Cheyenne, and Ho-Chunk women all played different versions of the game. In this version of the game two balls were attached to each other with a leather thong. Among the Arapaho, a girl would hold the thong in her hand while throwing and catching the ball. Cheyenne women held the 24-inch thong in their hands and kicked the ball. Their goal was to kick the ball as many times as possible without missing. In the Cheyenne game the ball had to be kicked without letting the ball or the player's foot touch the ground. In the Ho-Chunk game, players had to make 100 successful kicks in order to win. When girls missed, their turn ended and they had to pass the foot bag to another player.

Indians of the Arctic and the Northwest played jackstraws, or pickup sticks. The Haida of the Northwest tossed sticks on a flat surface and then tried to remove one at a time from the pile without moving any of the other sticks. The Inuit people of the western part of what is now Alaska used a small wooden hook to remove the sticks from the pile where they had fallen. The Inuit also developed another game with the sticks. A player would place a bundle of 50 to 75 sticks on the back of his or her hand. After quickly removing the hand, the player would then try to grasp as many sticks as possible before they fell to the ground.

GAMES OF STRATEGY

Indians of North America played guessing games. The most commonly played guessing game was a hand game. In most versions players moved two small sticks that they had marked from hand to hand in front of their opponents. They moved them quickly and in ways that would confuse the other players, who had to guess which stick was in which hand. Often drum music and singing accompanied these games.

The Anishinabe and the Menominee, who lived in the Great Lakes region of the Northeast, played a guessing game called the moccasin game. Four players sat at opposite sides of a blanket. Each team took turns hiding four game pieces beneath four moccasins while the opposing team watched. One of the pieces was marked. The watchers had to figure out under which moccasin the marked piece was hidden. Both hand games and the moccasin game helped to sharpen players' power of observation and ability to hide their feelings in order to keep a straight face.

Indians throughout the Americas played board games. The games of the Maya and Aztec of Mesoamerica are best known today. One of these games was called *patolli*. *Patolli* boards were scratched into stone building floors and on benches in Aztec cities. Most often patolli was played on a marked board or paper. Players used beans for counters. *Patolli* was similar to backgammon or Parcheesi. The first person to travel around the board and safely return home was the winner.

The Maya also played a game called *bul*. They used grains of corn for markers and used other grains of corn that had been burned on one side as dice. Players advanced their markers by throwing the dice. If they landed on a space occupied by another player's marker or "warrior," they could capture it, then change direction to drag it back to the other end of the board. At that point the opponent's warrior would be officially dead. The game ended when one player lost

Indians playing the board game *patolli*. **This drawing is from** *Historia de las cosas de Nuevo España* **by Bernardo Sahagún.** *(Library of Congress, Rare Books Division)*

all of his or her warriors. When more than two people played, the rules were more complicated. Some Maya still play a version of the game today. Like the game of chess that Europeans played, *bul* required thinking and strategy, two skills that were important for leaders and warriors.

Weapons and Armor

American Indians developed many types of weapons and armor. They used these weapons to attack and to defend themselves against enemies. In addition to carrying shields, Indians also wore special clothing that protected their bodies against injury when they were fighting.

WEAPONS AND ARMOR OF NORTH AMERICA

The earliest weapons that Indians of North America made were clubs. Mound Builders of the Mississippi Valley sometimes carved these clubs from one large piece of stone. Many other Indians made clubs by lashing a heavy stone onto a wooden handle with wet rawhide. When the hide dried, it held the stone tightly in place. Indians of the Northeast made a war club by carving a piece of heavy wood so that it had a knob on the striking end.

The word *tomahawk* comes from the Algonquian word *tamahak*. It meant a stone-headed weapon with a handle. Some tribes used

ARROWS

American Indians used arrows shaped like triangles for war. Often they loosely fixed arrow points to their shafts. When the wounded person tried to pull the arrow out, the shaft would come off and the point would remain lodged in the person's body. Sometimes Indian arrow makers also scratched grooves into their arrows, so that blood would more easily flow from the wounds they made.

copper-tipped arrows, but Indians of the Americas did not make weapons from iron. Europeans traded metal-bladed tomahawks to the Indians of North America in exchange for furs. The most popular ones were made to be used as weapons and as pipes. Indians of the Northeast and the Great Plains smoked pipes filled with tobacco during peacemaking ceremonies. Some tribes buried their weapons in the ground when they made peace. This is why people today say that they *bury the hatchet* to mean that they have stopped arguing.

Indians of North America also fought with sharp spears. They made the points for their spears by chipping them from flint and

This Iroquois man is carrying a war club in his left hand. He has a tomahawk in his belt and a tomahawk pipe in his right hand. Indians obtained metal tomahawks from Europeans through trade. Traditional tomahawks had blades of stone. This drawing, like many of the 1700s, showed Indians as savages. Many colonists believed Indian people to be inferior to themselves. *(Library of Congress, Prints and Photographs Division [LC-USZC2-1664])*

obsidian, stones that can be flaked to a razor-sharp edge. Indians of the Great Lakes, the Mississippi River Valley, and parts of what is now Florida made copper spear points. In addition to spears, Indians made knives from stone, shell, bone, horn, and copper. When they could find it, Indians used iron from meteors to make knives.

Before they invented bows and arrows, Indians threw sharp darts through the air using atlatls. An atlatl is a board that is about 18 inches long. It has a groove along the top where a spear rests. The end of the spear handle is loosely fixed onto the board with a hook. To use an atlatl, a warrior held onto the throwing board by the opposite end from the hook. He (most warriors were men) held it over his shoulder and then quickly moved his arm forward so that the dart would fly through the air. Atlatls are effective weapons because the darts that they launch have 200 times the power of darts that are thrown by hand.

Later North American Indians used bows for fighting and hunting. Most often these bows were made from a single piece of wood. They were about five to six feet long. Indians of some tribes reinforced their bows with thin pieces of sinew. These bows were about three and a half feet long—shorter than bows made from wood alone. Sinew backing gave bows about three

▲▼▲▼▲▼▲▼▲▼▲▼▲▼▲▼▲▼▲▼▲▼▲▼▲▼▲

COUNTING COUP

Indians of the Great Plains used clubs, but they also developed another way of fighting that was not so dangerous. They carried a curved stick that was specially decorated and tried to touch the enemy with it. When the French fur traders saw this they called it counting coup. (*Coup* means a blow in French.) Indians of the Plains believed that it was better to touch an enemy with a stick than to kill that person. One had to get close enough to make physical contact but without using a weapon. This could be very dangerous, and so was considered brave. Later, when horses were introduced to the Plains, Indians stole horses from their enemies in order to humiliate them. Coup counting and horse stealing allowed Indians to settle many disputes without the loss of life.

▼▲▼▲▼▲▼▲▼▲▼▲▼▲▼▲▼▲▼▲▼▲▼▲▼▲▼

times the power of bows without it. Indians of the Arctic, Plains, Great Basin, Plateau, Northwest, and California all made sinew-backed bows at the time of European contact.

The Hidatsa and the Shoshone sometimes made bows of horn. They softened large mountain sheep's horns by heating them. Then they shaped them and put two of them together to form a bow shape. They held the horns together with pieces of sinew. Horn bows were very strong.

To protect themselves against battle injuries, some Indians of the Southeast wore breastplates that they made from the rib bones of animals. They also wore armor over their chests made from pieces of cane, tall plants with thick stems. They tied the pieces together with strips of leather. Some wore wooden breastplates and carried shields. Many Indian warriors of the Southeast wore shells around their necks to protect their throats from arrows.

Indians of the Northeast also wore armor made from wooden slats that they had tied together. Some Indians of the Northeast carried wooden shields. The Anishinabe Indians (Chippewa) who lived in what is now the Midwest made shields from rawhide. Rawhide is animal skin that has not been treated to soften it.

The two American Indian men in this picture are dressed for war. They are from the Northeast and carry shields, bows, and arrows. This drawing was first published in 1619. *(Library of Congress, Prints and Photographs Division [LC-USZ62-98768])*

Plains Indians also made rawhide shields from elk or buffalo hide. The Mandan people of what is now North Dakota used the thick hide from a buffalo's neck for their shields. They made the shields even stronger by boiling buffalo hooves to make glue that they painted on their shields. This glue hardened when it dried.

In the Southwest the earliest Pueblo people, who were expert basket makers, wove armor out of plant fibers. They carried woven shields as well. Later they made and carried large, round rawhide shields.

Indians of the Plateau and the Northwest protected themselves by wearing armor that they made from wooden slats. They also carried shields that they made by tying wooden slats together. Some Indians of the Northwest made thick ropes from cedar bark and wrapped them around their bodies to protect themselves from injury. The chiefs of some Northwest tribes, including the Tinglit, wore wooden helmets that covered their necks.

▲▼▲▼▲▼▲▼▲▼▲▼▲▼▲▼▲▼▲▼▲▼▲▼▲▼▲

HIDE SHIRTS

Several tribes of North American Indians protected themselves against chest wounds by wearing vests or shirts made from five to six layers of animal hides. Moose and elk hides were often used because they were thick but flexible. Indians who wore this type of armor included the Assiniboine of the Great Plains and the Navajo (Dineh) of the Southwest.

▼▲▼▲▼▲▼▲▼▲▼▲▼▲▼▲▼▲▼▲▼▲▼▲▼▲▼

In what is now California the Pomo Indians wore vests that they made from willow or hazel shoots that they wove together with plant fiber cords. Some of these vests were two layers thick.

To make armor some Indians of the Subarctic glued pebbles onto their hide shirts with pitch, a sticky substance that comes from trees. The Inuit of the Arctic stitched together ivory chest protectors with pieces of sinew. They obtained the ivory from walrus tusks.

WEAPONS AND ARMOR OF MESOAMERICA

Indians of Mesoamerica used a variety of weapons. When the Mesoamerican soldiers were close to their enemies they used clubs, spears, and swords. Some of the wooden clubs that Mesoamerican soldiers fought with looked like paddles. They were covered with sharp stone blades set into slots. Other clubs resembled those that North American Indians used. They had a ball at the end and were designed to deliver a crushing blow to an enemy.

They also used swords made from wood with stone blades fit into grooves on both sides. These blades were held in place with strong glue. The biggest Aztec swords were as tall as a man and about four inches wide. (Aztec men were about 5'6" tall.) Aztec soldiers used both hands when they fought with them. According to the Spaniards, these swords were so sharp that an Aztec soldier could cut the head from a horse with one blow.

Mesoamerican Indians also fought with atlatls. They used copper and fish bone as well as chipped stone for dart tips. Some of their

TRIBUTE

The Aztec received arrows as tribute from the city-states that they conquered as they built their empire. They made certain that all of these arrows were made in the same way and were exactly the same size. The uniform size and design made it easier for Aztec archers to hit their mark.

This page is from the *Huexotzinco Codex*, an Aztec book that was written in 1531. It is a written record of military tribute that city-state rulers were expected to pay to the Aztec Empire. The drawings of soldiers show how common soldiers dressed. *(Harkness Collection, Manuscript Division, Library of Congress)*

darts had barbs or hooks on them. Barbed darts could not be pulled from a wound. Instead, they had to be cut out. Some of the darts that Mesoamerican warriors made had two or three prongs. They hardened the wooden shafts of their atlatl darts by heating them in a fire. According to Spaniards, a dart thrown with an atlatl could pierce metal armor and kill a conquistador.

Mesoamerican warriors also threw rocks at their enemies with slings. A sling is a long piece of leather or cord that is wider in the middle than at the ends. A soldier using a sling put a rock into the sling, twirled the sling in a circle over his head and then released one end of it. The rock flew through the air quickly and with great power. Some conquistadores reported that stones launched with slings wounded Spaniards wearing metal armor.

The soldiers of Mesoamerica made bows from curved pieces of wood and bowstrings from strips of deer hide. The arrows that they used when they fought were different than those that they used for hunting. War arrows that were shaped from flint or obsidian were sometimes barbed. Others were blunt. Blunt arrows were meant to stun or injure an enemy rather than kill him. Conquistadores reported that some Aztec archers were such good shots that they could shoot three arrows at the same time.

To protect themselves, Aztec warriors of high rank wore vests on their chests that were made of many layers of cotton, which was quilted, or sewn together in several places. These vests were about an inch thick. A Spaniard, Diego de Landa, wrote in the 1600s that Aztec soldiers dipped their vests in salt water and let them dry. By doing this several times they made the cotton more difficult to pierce. Because his is the only mention of this practice, many historians believe that he confused the Aztec word for *salt* with that for *tie*, since both words sound similar.

In addition to cotton armor Aztec soldiers of high rank wore leather or gold protectors on their lower legs. On their feet they wore sandals. They also wore wooden helmets. Some of these were carved to look like animal heads. Often they were covered with bird feathers. To protect their bodies against arrows and spears, warriors carried shields. Some were square and some were circular. Many shields were made of pieces of thick reed that were tied together with fiber from maguey cactus plants. The Aztec made other shields from wood. The shields that Aztec nobles carried were covered with painted hide or colorful feathers.

Common soldiers of the Aztec and other Mesoamerican armies wore only rough loincloths that were woven from maguey cactus fibers. They fought without shoes, cotton armor, or any other protection. They painted their bodies with pigments in the colors that symbolized the units to which they belonged. Archaeologists have found rollers that they believe may have been used to apply body paint.

WEAPONS AND ARMOR OF SOUTH AMERICA

Inca soldiers of South America used many of the same weapons as the Aztec did. These weapons included clubs, spears, slings, and bows and arrows. Like Mesoamerican soldiers did, they made copper tips for their arrows and spears.

The Inca fought with a heavy pointed stone that was attached to a wooden handle. The six points radiated outward and were designed to crush bones. Sometimes weapon makers used metal to form the striking part of this club instead of stone. They cast these metal club heads by pouring molten (melted) bronze into a mold and letting it cool. Bronze is a mixture of the metals copper and tin.

Unlike the Aztec army, the Inca army issued all of its soldiers protective clothing. To prevent injury on the battlefield, Inca soldiers wore padded vests made from cotton or from llama wool. Some of them protected their heads with padded cotton helmets, others with wooden helmets. They carried round or square wooden shields that were covered with metal or deer hide. To protect their backs, they wore woven mats. They wore round metal disks on the front of their chests and on the back. These disks were made of bronze, silver, or gold and were made to show the military honors that the soldier had earned rather than for protection. They served the same purpose as modern military medals.

▲▼▲▼▲▼▲▼▲▼▲▼▲▼▲▼▲▼▲▼▲▼▲▼▲▼▲▼▲▼

BOLAS

As the Inca empire expanded, the government drafted soldiers for its army from the territories that it conquered. These soldiers were experts at using the types of weapons that were most used where they lived. For example, some Inca soldiers used bolas, a bundle of three cords tied to rocks. The soldier held a weighted cord and twirled the other weighted cords overhead. When he threw the bola, the weights spun in a circle. When they were aimed at an enemy soldier's legs, the bola strings would wrap around them and cause the soldier to fall to the ground.

▼▲▼▲▼▲▼▲▼▲▼▲▼▲▼▲▼▲▼▲▼▲▼▲▼▲▼▲▼▲▼

Inca army officers wore more elaborately decorated clothing. Their helmets were covered with bird feathers, gold, and precious stones. Often their weapons were covered with gold. The officers also wore tunics of brightly colored cloth. The color of these tunics symbolized the unit to which the officer belonged and helped soldiers sort out who was who on the battlefield.

Indians who lived in the Amazon Basin of South America did not fight using large armies as the Inca did. When they fought other tribes they used bows and arrows, stone knives, and spears. They also fought with wooden clubs. They made spikes on these clubs by setting the points of animal horns into them.

Amazon Indian warriors are best known today for making blowguns, hollow tubes designed for shooting darts. They blew through one end of the wooden tube to shoot a dart at an enemy. Blowgun makers of the Amazon Basin fitted two equal lengths of hardwood together to form a tube. They smoothed the inside of the tube so that the dart would hit its target accurately.

Hunters of the Amazon Basin tipped the darts for their blowguns with curare. *Curare* means "poison" in Carib, a language spoken in the Amazon Basin. They made curare from the roots of the curare plant, a large vine that grows on trees in the tropical rain forest. The natural poison in this plant is called D-turbocurarine. It works by interrupting the signals from the brain to the muscles, so that an enemy cannot move. If enough curare enters a person's bloodstream the muscles of the chest will be paralyzed and he or she will die from suffocation.

Indians of the Amazon mixed other poisons with those of the curare plant to coat their dart points. Different groups of Indians had different recipes for the poisons they made. They added other poisonous plants and the venom from poisonous snakes and frogs. To make the poison for their arrows, they boiled these ingredients in water until they were thick syrup. Tribes of Indians who made the strongest poison traded it with other Indians for goods that they needed.

Indians of the Amazon also poisoned darts by heating them and rubbing them on the backs of golden poison frogs. These tiny, bright yellow frogs secrete a poison called batrachotoxin that prevents other animals from eating them. Once the darts had been treated, they could be stored for up to two years and remain powerful.

8 ◆ **Military Tactics**

American Indians used offensive and defensive military strategies against other Indians that they considered their enemies. Military strategy is the art of planning a battle. Some of the techniques that Indians of North America developed for fighting were so effective that the European colonists used them to defeat the British soldiers during the American Revolution.

Mesoamerican Aztec generals and South American Inca generals were masters of military strategy. They were experts at moving soldiers into the battlefield and keeping them supplied. Their armies were highly organized and highly trained.

NORTH AMERICAN MILITARY STRATEGY

North American Indians sometimes raided other tribes for food or took captives. Such battles were a way for young men to show their bravery. They also were a reaction to an insult from another tribe. Fighting was a part of life for most North American Indians, but it was not a way of life.

Indian people knew the land where they lived. They used this knowledge to their advantage. From hunting, they knew how to travel quietly and how to keep from being seen. Instead of marching close together, they spaced themselves out and traveled in single file to keep from being noticed and from being targets. They used these skills to stalk human enemies and to ambush them, hiding until the enemy came close and then attacking them.

North American Indians were also experts at raiding. They sent out scouts in order to gather information on the enemy. Warriors

Some tribes of American Indians of the Northeast built tall log fences around their villages in order to protect them against enemies. These fences are called stockades. This engraving was made between 1590 and 1598. *(Library of Congress, Prints and Photographs Division [LC-USZ62-367])*

then suddenly appeared in the enemy camp and began to fight. After the fight was over, they retreated just as quickly. All of these fighting methods are known today as guerrilla warfare. *Guerrilla* is a Spanish word that means a small independent group of soldiers.

When the colonists arrived in North America and began killing Indians in order to take their land, Indian people's lives became centered on fighting for survival. The colonists forced North American Indians to move to places that were home or hunting grounds for other tribes. As land and food became scarce, tribes began to fight one another. At the same time they had to defend themselves against the Europeans.

▲▼▲▼▲▼▲▼▲▼▲▼▲▼▲▼▲▼▲▼▲▼▲▼▲▼▲▼▲

LIVING WITH THE INDIANS

Some captives refused to return to their white relatives. Historians who studied 1,206 New England Indian captives taken between 1675 and 1763 learned that one in five chose to stay with their Indian captors. Although some of the men refused to be ransomed, most of the captives who remained with the Indians were women. This trend continued as the frontier moved west. Examples of this are Cynthia Ann Parker, who became the mother of Comanche war leader Quanak Parker, and Mary Jemison.

▼▲▼▲▼▲▼▲▼▲▼▲▼▲▼▲▼▲▼▲▼▲▼▲▼▲▼▲▼

Instead of fighting to kill as many of the enemy as they could, North American warriors often settled scores by humiliating their enemies. One way of doing this was to take captives. Some tribes brought captives home and gave them to families who had lost loved ones in the battle. This helped provide another worker/hunter/provider to families who had lost one. Although certain groups of Indians treated the captives as slaves, many others adopted the captives into the family and the tribe, treating them as relatives.

American Indians took captives as part of their fighting strategy. They exchanged captives for guns, gunpowder, other weapons, and money. This drawing that was made in 1833 shows Sauk and Fox Indians with three captives taken during the Black Hawk War of 1832, fought in what is now northern Illinois. *(Library of Congress, Prints and Photographs Division [LC-USZ62-39381])*

When Indians fought with non-Indians, taking captives was a good way for them to get guns, powder, metal swords, and metal knives, as well as money to buy other supplies that they needed. They held captives for ransom, insisting that their white enemies buy them back.

Unlike Indians, European soldiers marched in close formation into unknown territory. Their bright military uniforms made them easy targets. North American Indians wore buckskin and paint to camouflage themselves. Even though lightning-fast strikes and quick retreats enabled Indians to win skirmishes and early battles against the colonists, the colonial generals called North American Indians "skulking Indians." They made fun of the Indian style of fighting and said it was disorganized and "ignoble."

Not until Europeans adopted the American Indian military techniques were they able to defeat the Indian people of North America

SCALPING

Scalping was not a normal part of North American Indian warfare before Europeans arrived. Scientists who study the past have found a few prehistoric skulls that show signs of cut marks, but they do not all agree that these marks are proof of scalping. If Indians practiced scalping, it was not widespread and was done rarely.

Colonial leaders paid bounties for scalps. In 1706 the governor of Pennsylvania offered 130 pieces of eight (a type of money) for the scalp of Indian men over 12 years of age and 50 pieces of eight for a woman's scalp. Those who paid the bounty could not tell victim's sex or age from a scalp. As a result, killing Indian women and children became a way for some colonists to make easy money. The Indians responded by scalping white women and children.

During the French and Indian Wars scalping was a common practice. The British and the French encouraged their Indian allies to scalp their enemies. They gave them metal scalping knives. Paying bounties for Indian scalps did not end in the United States until the 1800s.

in battle. Some of the strategies and battle plans devised by indigenous warriors are still taught today at the U.S. Military Academy at West Point.

MESOAMERICAN MILITARY STRATEGY

Many of the people of Mesoamerica lived in city-states made up of a city and a small area of land around it. Each city-state had a ruler and an army. Some of the rulers formed alliances with other cities so that they could better defend against attack. These armies also fought against other city-states. Although wars between city-states were frequent, they tended to be small.

This changed when the Aztec (Mexica) moved to the central valley of what is now Mexico in about A.D. 1100 and started to expand their empire. The Aztec rulers decided which city-states to conquer based on what goods they could obtain from them. First they conquered the smallest ones to make an example of them. Then they declared war against more powerful city-states. By this time these larger city-states no longer had allies, so they were easier to defeat.

The easiest way for the Aztec to expand their empire was to frighten city-states into giving up without fighting. To do this they needed a large, well-trained army. Every male who could fight was expected to serve. The sons of common people began their training when they were six or seven years old by attending military schools called *telpochcalli*. Each district of Tenochtitlán, the Aztec capital, had its own school. Young boys were given jobs to do, such as building fires and sweeping. They also studied how to use weapons. They began their combat experience by carrying the shields of soldiers in battle. The sons of noble families attended another school called a *calmecac*. They learned how to become leaders.

When young men were 20 years old, they were apprenticed to a veteran who looked after them in battle. After a young man first captured an enemy soldier without any help, he was called a leading youth. When soldiers had taken four captives, they became veteran warriors. In addition to honors, Az-

▲▽▲▽▲▽▲▽▲▽▲▽▲▽▲▽▲▽▲▽▲▽▲▽▲▽▲▽▲▽▲

TAKING CAPTIVES

The goal of Aztec fighting was to capture soldiers rather than kill them in battle. The captives were used as sacrifices in Aztec religious ceremonies.

▼▲▼▲▼▲▼▲▼▲▼▲▼▲▼▲▼▲▼▲▼▲▼▲▼▲▼▲▼▲▼

The type of feathers that an elite Aztec soldier used on his helmet and shield showed his rank and duties. During battle an Aztec commander and his troops dressed in the same colors, so that it was easy to tell one unit apart from the other. They also carried flags to identify their units. The original manuscript from which this drawing comes was written by Fray Diego Durán in 1585. *(Peter Force Collection, Manuscript Division, Library of Congress)*

tec soldiers also received gifts from the emperor for taking captives. The higher in rank a soldier was, the more armor he could wear. Common soldiers wore only loincloths and body paint.

In battle Aztec officers divided the soldiers they commanded into smaller units in order to attack the enemy from many sides. Sometimes the Aztec troops pretended to run away in order to lead their opponents into an ambush. When the enemy soldiers chased after them, hidden Aztec soldiers would attack them from the sides and the rear.

Aztec soldiers often used trench warfare. They dug ditches, covered them with brush, and hid in them until the enemy passed by. Then they jumped out for a surprise attack. When necessary, the Aztec army traveled over the water in rafts to sneak up on their enemies. When an enemy fortress was on a high mountain with steep sides, Aztec military engineers designed and made ladders in the battlefield, so that the troops could enter the city.

Once a city-state had been conquered, the Aztec drew up surrender documents containing the amount of tribute the city-state

▲▽▲▽▲▽▲▽▲▽▲▽▲▽▲▽▲▽▲▽▲▽▲▽▲▽▲▽

SPIES

Spies gave the Aztec officers useful information that they could employ against their enemies in battle. Sometimes merchants worked as spies. Since traders were allowed to travel freely throughout Mesoamerica, they could secretly learn a great deal about other city-states. The Aztec also sent out spies who dressed in the clothing of the people they were spying on and who traveled at night to avoid being caught. The Aztec emperor gave successful spies land and other gifts. Unsuccessful spies did not live very long.

▽▲▽▲▽▲▽▲▽▲▽▲▽▲▽▲▽▲▽▲▽▲▽▲▽▲▽

had to pay them. One tribute the defeated city-states were required to pay was to supply the Aztec army with food and weapons when they marched through the area. This allowed the Aztec army to travel without being burdened by supplies. The Aztec emperor then chose one of his nobles to serve as the new ruler.

MILITARY STRATEGY OF SOUTH AMERICA

The Inca army was also well trained and organized. It was so large that as many as 200,000 soldiers served in its ranks. These soldiers did not all serve at once. Instead, many of them were reserves. Most of the soldiers of the Inca army came from territories that the Inca had conquered. Military service was part of their *mit'a*, or work tax. They lived in their own homes in their villages and were required to participate in regular military drills. These training exercises prepared them to fight when the emperor ordered them to battle.

The smallest group of Inca soldiers was made up of 10 men. Their leader was called The Guardian of Ten. It was his job to train his men, feed them, and provide them with weapons. The Guardian of Fifty looked after five smaller units. He inspected the troops beneath his command to make certain they were well armed and well trained. Officers, who were part of the Inca nobility, were in charge of units of 100; 1,000; 2,500; and 10,000 men.

The Inca emperor handpicked the commander of the army, usually his close relative. During battle the Inca emperor also served as supreme commander. Soldiers carried him to the battlefield on a litter, a chair supported by poles. During the fighting, he stayed at the rear, surrounded by his most trusted soldiers.

The Inca army marched over the stone roads built throughout the empire. While they were marching, they stopped at garrisons to rest. These stone barracks were spaced a day's travel apart from each other. Warehouses that contained food and weapons were also spaced along the roads, so that the Inca army could be easily supplied. When the soldiers left the borders of the empire to travel where there were no warehouses, they used pack trains of llamas to carry supplies to them.

Many times the sight of the enormous army was enough to inspire Inca enemies to surrender. Those that did not give up faced a difficult fight. The Inca army's main goal was to capture the leader of the opposing army. They tried to

▲▼▲▼▲▼▲▼▲▼▲▼▲▼▲▼▲▼▲▼▲▼▲▼▲▼▲

MILITARY DISCIPLINE
According to Inca law, if a soldier left the road to commit a crime against a citizen of the Inca Empire, he was put to death. The Inca military had similar punishments for other undisciplined acts soldiers might commit.

▼▲▼▲▼▲▼▲▼▲▼▲▼▲▼▲▼▲▼▲▼▲▼▲▼▲▼

do this as quickly as possible. Sometimes Inca officers divided their troops into three groups. One division attacked the enemy soldiers head on while two other groups secretly marched on either side of the battle so that they could attack the enemy from the rear. Another tactic was to use soldiers to split the enemy army in half so that they could weaken it.

When an enemy tried to retreat, the Inca soldiers set fire to dry grass on the battlefield to stop them. If the opposing soldiers managed to retreat to a stone fortress, once they were inside, the Inca cut off their food and water supplies. Sometimes the soldiers keeping this siege would pretend to leave. As soon as the enemy soldiers came out of their fortress, one division of Inca troops would appear to block their escape while another division took over the fortress.

A NEW KIND OF FIGHTING

Given the fighting skills of American Indians, it is difficult to imagine how Europeans could have taken over their land. According to modern military historians, one of the major reasons that European forces won in their battles with Indians was that the colonists and conquistadores brought new diseases to the Americas. Because American Indians had never been exposed to European diseases, their immune systems had not developed resistance to these diseases.

As measles, smallpox, typhoid, and influenza (flu) swept through the Americas, millions of Indians sickened and died. Many Indian people died before they had a chance to even see the colonizers who carried the germs with them from Europe. By the early

In this old engraving, colonists are shown attacking a fortified Indian village of the Northeast and killing women and children. Attacks such as these provoked Indian people to fight back in kind. *(Library of Congress, Prints and Photographs Division [LC-USZ62-049750])*

▲▼▲▼▲▼▲▼▲▼▲▼▲▼▲▼▲▼▲▼▲▼▲▼▲▼▲▼▲

GERM WARFARE

In the French and Indian Wars the British may have used smallpox as germ warfare against the Indians. Jeffrey, Lord Amherst, commander of the British forces in North America, wrote from Fort Pitt to an officer under his command: "I will try to inoculate the Indians by means of Blankets that may fall in their hands, taking care however not to get the disease myself. As it is pity to oppose good men against them, I wish we could make use of the Spaniard's Method, and hunt them with English Dogs. Supported by Rangers, and some Light Horse, who would I think effectively extirpate or remove that Vermin." (The Spanish conquistadores routinely used attack dogs to kill Indians and tear them limb from limb.) There is no concrete evidence that this plan was carried out, but it very likely was put into practice.

▼▲▼▲▼▲▼▲▼▲▼▲▼▲▼▲▼▲▼▲▼▲▼▲▼▲▼▲▼

1600s about 90 percent of the Indian population of the Americas had died from European diseases.

During the earliest battles between Europeans and Indians, the colonists and conquistadores had another important advantage because their spears were made of iron and steel. Iron and steel weapons were harder and lasted longer than stone- or copper-tipped arrows. Until American Indians adopted the horses that Europeans reintroduced to the Americas, mounted European soldiers had another big military advantage against the Indians. They could move faster than soldiers on foot.

Guns were also a help to the earliest colonists and conquistadores. North American Indians readily obtained guns from fur traders. American Indians quickly became expert sharpshooters. Despite their skill at using guns and keeping them in working order, they were not able to manufacture them or able to obtain as many guns as the Europeans possessed. Cannons were very difficult for Indians to obtain.

The Indian people were shocked at first by the bloody battles mounted by the Europeans. Killing enemies was not the main goal of

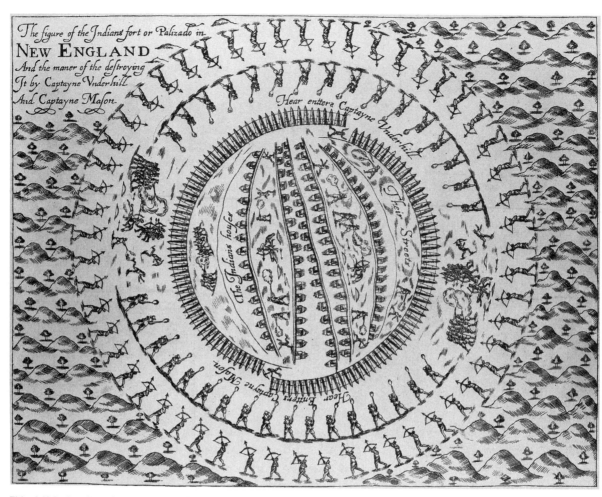

This 1638 drawing shows colonial English captains Underhill and Mason and their soldiers destroying a Pequot village in 1637. Seven hundred Indian people, including women and children, died in this attack. The Pequot lived in what is now Connecticut. The Narragansett Indians shown behind the colonial soldiers, fought on the side of the English, against the Pequot. *(Library of Congress, Prints and Photographs Division [LC-USZ62-32055])*

most fighting that Indians did. For Indian people any sort of fighting was usually a last resort to resolve arguments between tribes. When they tried talking with the Europeans in order to come to an agreement, they expected the conquistadores and colonizers to keep their word, but the Europeans did not. By the 1800s disease, combined with waves of European immigration, had taken their toll. At the start of the Sioux Wars in the mid-1800s, Europeans outnumbered Indians in the American West by 10 to one.

9

Military Contributions

Indians of the Americas fought to protect their families and homes from European invaders. They resisted giving up their land and their way of life. When Indian leaders' efforts to cooperate failed, some tried to drive the colonists away. Many American Indians fought against colonizers. Others joined with Europeans against colonists and tribes that they considered enemies. Many American Indians volunteered to fight for the French and the British during the French and Indian Wars.

After the United States and Canadian governments were established, American Indians enlisted in the U.S. and Canadian armies. Beginning with the French and Indian Wars, North American Indian soldiers have risked their lives in military service to their country. Many have died. Today an estimated 190,000 American Indian veterans live in the United States.

FIGHTING AGAINST EUROPEAN AMERICANS

Indian people won many individual battles against colonists and conquistadores, although they did not stop the Europeans in the end. Little Turtle, the war leader of the Miami Indians, a tribe in the Midwest, defeated the U.S. Army in a battle in 1791. The battle took place about 50 miles from present-day Ft. Wayne, Indiana. About 1,000 Miami and Shawnee Indians fought under Little Turtle against 1,300 soldiers led by General Arthur St. Clair, who was the governor of the Northwest Territory. The U.S. soldiers had been sent to punish the Indians for raiding settlements on land that the Indians still considered theirs.

Red Cloud, leader of the Oglala Lakota Sioux, waged a long-term war against the U.S. Army. The army, under orders from the U.S. government, was attempting to force the Lakota people to give up their land and live on reservations. *(National Archives at College Park/Photograph No. NWDNS-111-SC-82537)*

American Indian soldiers outnumbered both French and British troops in many battles of the French and Indian Wars.

Little Turtle's warriors killed about 600 of St. Clair's men and wounded about 300 more. Only 66 Indians were killed in the fighting. Some historians consider this battle to be the worst defeat the U.S. Army ever suffered.

In 1866 the Lakota (Sioux) leader, Red Cloud, fought the most successful long-term war against the United States by an Indian tribe. Red Cloud and his soldiers attacked forts that the U.S. Army had built along the Bozeman Trail. This trail ran through Lakota land. Gold miners and settlers used it. Red Cloud's warriors defeated Lieutenant Colonel William Fetterman's soldiers near Fort Phil Kearny in what is now Wyoming in 1866. The Lakota continued to attack forts. By 1868, the defeated U.S. government decided to sign the Fort Laramie Treaty. In it the United States agreed to give up its forts on the Bozeman Trail. The Lakota were allowed to keep the western part of what are now South Dakota and part of Wyoming and Montana. Later the United States broke this treaty.

FIGHTING BESIDE EUROPEAN AMERICANS

French and British military commanders in the Northeast asked the help of American Indians to fight the French and Indian Wars in the mid-1700s. First French and then British generals used Indians whom they considered friendly to serve as scouts. Later they asked these Indians to fight with them against other Indians and their European-American enemies.

French and Indian Wars

The French and Indian Wars were fought between British and French troops in North America. They lasted from 1754 to 1763. The two countries fought to decide which one would control the eastern part of what is now Canada and the northeastern part of what would become the United Sates. The French asked Algonquian-speaking Indian tribes to help them by raiding the English. The tribes of the

Ohio Valley also helped the French. During the early part of the fighting the Iroquois Confederacy tried to remain neutral, but later they supported the British. The Iroquois Confederacy was made up of the Cayuga, Mohawk, Oneida, Onondaga, Seneca, and later the Tuscarora nations.

American Indians influenced the outcome of the French and Indian Wars. In one battle the British sent General Braddock to attack Ft. Duquesne near Pittsburgh, Pennsylvania. They marched down the road to battle in long rows of men, three abreast. This was the way that Europeans had always marched. They did not see the French and Indians who were hiding in the surrounding woods until it was too late. Each time British soldiers tried to run for cover their officers stopped them. The British were defeated in this battle but eventually they won the war.

Revolutionary War

The Revolutionary War was fought from 1775 to 1783 between England and the Continental army of the 13 colonies. Most of the American Indians who fought in this war did so for the British. These tribes included the Creek, Cherokee, and many members of the Iroquois League. Mohawk chief Joseph Brant and 1,500 members of the Iroquois Confederacy fought beside the British Royal Regiment. The Tuscarora and Oneida did not take sides.

Many Indians fought for the British because they had made treaties with them. The Indian people believed that if the British won, they could keep the land that remained to them under these treaties.

The colonial government had a reputation for taking Indian land and Indian lives. For the most part, the colonists did not try to convince Indians to fight with them. Instead they told the Indian tribes that the war was a family fight and urged them to stay out of it.

General George Washington wanted to use Indians to help fight the British. In 1778 he wrote, "I think they can be made of excellent use, as scouts and light troops." The Mohican and Stockbridge Indians fought with Washington for independence from the British. They also fought at Bunker Hill and in many other battles.

War of 1812

After the American Revolution, the new U.S. government began making treaties with Indian tribes. The first treaties were with the

Tyonajanen, an Oneida woman who was married to a Continental army officer, rode with him in at least one battle. Mounted on a horse, she rode by his side and loaded his gun for him after he suffered a wound to the wrist.

Cherokee. The United States also signed treaties with the Chickasaw, Choctaw, and Creek. The treaty of Ft. Wayne, Indiana, gave the United States title to, or legal ownership of, 3 million acres of Indian land for a payment of eight cents an acre.

Tecumseh, a Shawnee leader, protested that because the chiefs who had signed the treaty did not own the land, they could not sell it. The U.S. government would not listen to him. Tecumseh then formed an alliance with the Chickasaw, Choctaw, and Creek. In 1811, while U.S. Army troops waited to attack the village that served as Tecumseh's headquarters, Indian troops attacked them first. The U.S. soldiers won the battle. Afterward they burned the village as well as the Indians' food.

When the United States declared war against the British in 1812, the army tried to talk the Indian tribes of Indiana Territory into joining them. Some agreed to this. Most did not believe the U.S. government to be a friend. They fought on the British side during the War of 1812. Tecumseh and his allies supported the British, helping them to take over the city of Detroit.

Stand Watie, a Cherokee general in the Confederate army, raised a cavalry unit that specialized in ambushing trains, steamships, and the Union army. He was the last Confederate general to surrender to the Union army. In all, about 4,000 Cherokee fought in the Confederate army. *(National Archives and Records Administration at College Park/Photograph No. NWDNS-111-B-4914)*

Civil War

Many American Indians fought on both sides during the Civil War. The Civil War lasted from 1861 to 1865. It was fought between the Union (the North) and the Confederacy (the South). The Confederacy counted the Creek, Choctaw, Quapaw, Seneca, and Osage as allies. The Cherokee did not take sides until pressure from a group led by Brigadier General Stand Watie, a Cherokee, convinced them to join the South's fight. More than 10,000 American Indians fought with the Confederate army.

About 3,600 Indians fought for the Union. Between 111 and 142 American Indian soldiers from the Oneida Reservation in Wisconsin served in the 14th Wisconsin Volunteer Infantry during the Civil War. Forty of them lost their lives fighting.

Iroquois soldiers made up the Tuscarora Company (D Company of the 132nd New York Volunteer Infantry) during the Civil War. Their

ELY PARKER

Ely Parker, a Seneca, served as an adjutant general, a division engineer, and secretary to Union general Ulysses S. Grant. As Grant's secretary, Parker copied the surrender terms that were signed by General Robert E. Lee at Appomattox Courthouse, Virginia, in 1865.

When Grant introduced his staff to Lee at Appomattox, the general shook each one's hand. He pulled back when he saw Parker. When he realized that Parker was an American Indian and not an African American, he reached out his hand and said, "I am glad to see one real American here." Parker told him, "We are all Americans."

Later Parker became the first American Indian to serve as U.S. commissioner on Indian Affairs. This was a cabinet-level position.

When he was 14 years old, Ely Parker served as scribe and interpreter for Seneca elders in their dealings with U.S. government officials. *(National Archives and Records Administration at College Park/ Photograph No. NWDNS-111-B-5272)*

leader was Lieutenant Cornelius C. Cusick, a peace chief of the Turtle Clan. He received a commission of second lieutenant after the war ended and spent the next 25 years in the U.S. Army.

Indian Wars in the West

As settlers pushed westward after the Civil War, the U.S. Army was ordered to move the Indian people from their land to reservations, pieces of land the government set aside for them. Often the Indians resisted. Fights between the Indians broke out in California, the Southwest, and the Great Plains. In July 1866 the U.S. Congress established the Indian Scouting Service and authorized the army to recruit 1,000 Indian scouts to help them win these battles. The next year army generals requested more than four times that number.

In the 1800s in the Southwest, U.S. Army officers used Hopi runners to carry messages to the railhead because they were faster and more reliable than their own troops.

Army commanders looked for scouts who were traditional enemies of the tribes that the United States was fighting. Unlike the Indian scouts who had worked with the army before, these new scouts were considered soldiers. The army paid them a salary. The army also trained them. If they broke rules, the army disciplined them. The Indian Scouting Service was an official part of the U.S. Army for 77 years.

After the Indian Wars had ended, American Indians from a number of tribes volunteered to serve in the U.S. Army. They served even though most had not been given citizenship. (American Indians were not all made citizens until 1924.) The army welcomed Indian soldiers.

Theodore Roosevelt actively recruited American Indians for his Rough Riders cavalry unit during the Spanish-American War in 1898. Four Lakota (Sioux) women who were nuns at Ft. Berthold, North Dakota, served as nurses in the Spanish-American War. One of them, who died of disease in Cuba, where they were stationed, was buried with military honors.

U.S. Army general John J. Pershing used 74 Apache scouts on his expedition into Mexico in 1916 to capture Pancho Villa. He commanded soldiers in the Mexican Revolution. He also made raids across the border into the United States.

▲▽▲▽▲▽▲▽▲▽▲▽▲▽▲▽▲▽▲▽▲▽▲▽▲▽▲▽▲▽▲

THE MEXICAN REVOLUTION

An army of Mesoamerican Indian soldiers followed popular leader Emiliano Zapata in Mexico between 1910 and 1919. Their goal was to take land from the rich landowners and return it to the peasant farmers. Zapata was part Indian. Indian people of Mexico consider him a hero today.

▽▲▽▲▽▲▽▲▽▲▽▲▽▲▽▲▽▲▽▲▽▲▽▲▽▲▽▲▽▲▽

World War I

World War I was fought in Europe beginning in 1914. Canadian troops landed in Europe that fall. At first the Canadian government tried to discourage American Indians from enlisting. By 1915 the government changed that policy. Canadian Indians volunteered in record numbers. According to the Canadian government, one in three able-bodied Indian men in that country enlisted. Cameron Brant, the great-great-grandson of Joseph Brant, commanded the 4th Canadian Infantry Battalion. He died in 1915 near Ypres, Belgium, when he led a counterattack into enemy trenches.

U.S. soldiers began fighting in the war in 1917. By the time the fighting in World War I ended in 1919, between 12,000 and 13,000 American Indians had joined the U.S. military. They made up between 20 and 30 percent of the American Indian adult male population. (About 15 percent of eligible non-Indian adult men served in the military in World War I.) American Indian soldiers served in the cavalry, the medical corps, and in military intelligence. They also served as engineers and military police. Fourteen American Indian women volunteered to serve in the Army Nurse Corps during World War I. Often

During World War I, American Indian soldiers from the Canadian Expeditionary Force pose with Indian elders for a group photo in 1916. *(Canadian Department of the Interior/National Archives of Canada/PA-041366)*

American Indian soldiers were placed in the most dangerous positions during battles. About 1 percent of all the soldiers in the American Expeditionary Forces died in battle. Five percent of the American Indian men in the American Expeditionary Forces died on the battlefield.

American Indians also served as code talkers. A code is a system of symbols, letters, or words that are used to transmit information secretly. During World War I, Choctaw soldiers in the U.S. Army's Thirty-sixth Division were chosen to be code talkers. They communicated with each other in their native Choctaw language. This kept messages secret from the Germans. At least one Choctaw soldier was placed in each field company headquarters. This soldier translated messages into the Choctaw language. Then he wrote them down so that runners could carry them to other companies. The German army was never able to crack the code.

World War II

World War II was fought from 1939 to 1945. It involved every major power in the world at the time. Most of the fighting in World War II took place in Europe, the Pacific Islands, and North Africa.

Canada entered this war in 1939. Government records show that 3,090 Indians volunteered for service, including 72 women. Some 2,500 Canadian Indians were drafted. The number of Canadian Indians who fought is much higher. The official count did not include Inuit and Métis volunteers. (The Métis are Canadian people with both American Indian and non-Indian ancestors.)

The United States entered the war at the end of 1941. During World War II more than 44,000 American Indians served in the U.S. military out of a total Indian population of less than 350,000. About 8,000 of that number were women. During World War II five American Indian soldiers earned the Medal of Honor, the U.S. military's highest honor.

Choctaw code talkers had been so successful in World War I that during World War II the U.S. Army used Choctaw code talkers again. They

▲▽▲▽▲▽▲▽▲▽▲▽▲▽▲▽▲▽▲▽▲▽▲▽▲▽▲▽▲

MISTAKEN IDENTITY

American Indian code talkers in the Pacific during World War II faced a special danger because many people mistook them for Japanese soldiers. In fact, at some points they were assigned bodyguards to avoid any confusion.

▼▲▼▲▼▲▼▲▼▲▼▲▼▲▼▲▼▲▼▲▼▲▼▲▼▲▼▲▼

The Navajo code talkers served in the U.S. Marines on Saipan in World War II. Code talkers could translate messages from their Navajo code into English in 20 seconds. Other codes that were not based on Indian languages took hours to translate. *Left to right:* Oscar Ilthma, Jack Nez, and Carl N. Gorman on Saipan in 1944. *(Department of Defense, U.S. Marine Corps/National Archives and Records Administration at College Park/Photograph No. NWDNS-127-N-82619)*

also used Comanche, Navajo (Dineh), and Dakota, Lakota, and Nakota Sioux soldiers as code talkers.

Twenty-nine Navajo soldiers were recruited to construct a written code from their language. They invented words that used nature to talk about military subjects, words to stand for each letter of the alphabet as well as other things, such as months of the year. For example, the Navajo word for potato meant "grenade," and Navajo code talkers called submarines "iron fish." They gave U.S. military units Navajo clan names. The Japanese were unable to break the code that the Navajo soldiers had invented.

By the end of the war, 420 Navajo had served in the code talker program with the Marines. The code talkers took part in every major assault the U.S. Marines conducted in the Pacific Theater from 1942 to

> Comanche code talkers used *posah-tai-vo,* or "crazy white man," to mean Adolf Hitler. For *bomber,* they made a phrase that was translated as "pregnant airplane."

1945. They communicated by field telephone and walkie-talkie to call in air strikes, direct troop movements, and report enemy locations.

American Indians also helped on the home front during World War II. They bought more than $50 million in war bonds. These bonds were issued by the government to help support the war effort. More than 40,000 American Indians left their homes to work in factories where they made tanks, airplanes, weapons, and munitions for the war.

Korean War, Vietnam War, and Beyond

The tradition of American Indian military service continued during the Korean War. American Indians served with U.S. forces in the Korean War, which lasted from 1950 to 1953. Ben Nighthorse Campbell, a Cheyenne, who is the first American Indian to serve in Congress since 1929, is a Korean War veteran. He served in the U.S. Air Force. Later American Indians served in what is called the Korean DMZ Border War fought between November 2, 1966, and October 18, 1969. The exact number of American Indians that served in this war is not known.

When U.S. troops fought in the Vietnam War between 1965 and 1973, once again, American Indians joined the military in record numbers. Of the 42,000 U.S. American Indians who served in Vietnam, nine out of 10 of them volunteered to serve. This is the highest record of voluntary service for any ethnic group. More than half of these American Indian soldiers served in combat.

Later American Indians served in the Persian Gulf War in 1991 and in the Iraq War in 2003. Private First Class Lori Piestewa, a Hopi from Arizona, was killed in Iraq in March 2003 when she and other soldiers were ambushed by enemy troops. She was the first American woman to die in Operation Iraqi Freedom, as this war was known, and the first known American Indian woman serving in the U.S. military to die in combat. Seven other soldiers were also killed in this ambush. Several were wounded including Pvt. Jessica Lynch. Piestewa, who had two young children, was from a family with a long military tradition. Her father was a Vietnam veteran and her grandfather was a World War II veteran.

When asked why Lori Piestewa and other American Indians serve in the military, Hopi tribal chairman Wayne Taylor, Jr., said, "[They] joined because of one reason that unites us all; they are Americans."

Diplomacy and Government

10

Indians of the Americas tried to resolve conflicts in order to avoid going to war. Solving disagreements by talking instead of fighting is called diplomacy. Indians also worked hard to find peaceful ways to solve conflicts between people within their own tribes. They selected leaders and established rules about how people should act.

Indians of the Americas made sure that everyone in their tribe had a job to do and a place to live. They also looked after those who needed help, sharing their food with their relatives and neighbors. North American Indians helped the first European colonists learn to farm on American soil because making certain that no one starved was their tradition. Indians of the Americas often gave gifts or tried to trade with the first Europeans they met. This was a way to have good relationships with people that they did not know. As Europeans began taking Indian lives and land, Indian people turned from diplomacy to fighting for their survival.

Many Europeans who came to the Americas believed that the Indian people who lived there were savages. Despite this belief, they borrowed Indian ideas about how to live together and get along. The U.S. Constitution contains many ideas created by the Iroquois Confederacy, an alliance of Northeast Indians. The idea that every child has a right to an education was part of the Aztec way of life. The Inca of South America had many social welfare programs that helped poor and disabled people until the conquistadores destroyed their system of government.

North American Indians held meetings called councils to make group decisions for their own people. They also met with non-Indians to make joint decisions and work through differences. Soon after contact, they discovered that non-Indians often broke agreements made in council meetings. This engraving made in 1810 shows Lewis and Clark meeting with Indians. *(Library of Congress, Prints and Photographs Division [LC-USZ62-73372])*

GOVERNMENTS OF NORTH AMERICA

In order to keep neighboring tribes from fighting, the Indian tribes of the Northeast formed alliances with one another. Two large nations of Huron gathered together to form a confederacy (an organized alliance) in about 1420. Later they were joined by two other nations. Each Huron nation kept its territory and traditions, but a confederacy council made decisions about war and trade. The council also settled disagreements between Huron nations that were part of the confederacy.

The Great Law of Peace

The Iroquois of the Northeast also formed a confederacy. Theirs was more formal than that of the Huron. The rules of this confederacy were called the Great Law of Peace. Today they are sometimes called the Iroquois Constitution. It was recorded on wampum belts—known as the Hiawatha belts—between A.D. 1000 and A.D. 1450.

This agreement joined the Iroquois nations of the Oneida, Onondaga, Mohawk, Cayuga, and the Seneca. Later the Tuscarora joined.

The Iroquois Constitution prevented government interference in people's daily lives. It also separated the civilian government from military and religious affairs. The Iroquois Constitution allowed religious freedom so that many different

▲▽▲▽▲▽▲▽▲▽▲▽▲▽▲▽▲▽▲▽▲▽▲▽▲▽▲▽

LISTENING

Unlike the government of England at the time, the Iroquois Confederacy held meetings that were very respectful. No one talked when someone else was speaking. In order for everyone to hear, the speakers sometimes used a megaphone to amplify their voices.

▼▲▽▲▽▲▽▲▽▲▽▲▽▲▽▲▽▲▽▲▽▲▽▲▽▲▽▲▽

Wampum belts that were made from purple and white shell beads recorded agreements between tribes that were part of the Iroquois Confederacy. Wampum belts were also used to declare war and to record history. In this photo from the 1870s Iroquois chiefs are shown reading wampum belts. *(Electric Studio/National Archives of Canada/ Photograph No. C-08137)*

Colonial leaders who created the blueprint for the U.S. government were influenced by principles set forth in the Iroquois Constitution when they wrote the U.S. Constitution. Here they sign the Declaration of Independence in 1776. *(Library of Congress, Prints and Photographs Division [LC-USZ62-3736])*

religions and faiths could exist side by side. Section 99 of the Iroquois Constitution stated: "[t]he rites and festivals [religious practices] of each nation shall remain undisturbed and shall continue as before because they were given by the people of old times as useful and necessary for the good of men."

Colonial leaders first found out about the Iroquois Constitution during treaty and council meetings they attended during the French and Indian War. In July 1744 at a meeting between the Indians and

the British, the Onondaga Chief Canassatego complained that it was almost impossible for the Iroquois to deal with the colonies. Each colony had its own government and way of doing things. He encouraged them to form a strong union and suggested that the colonists use the Iroquois Constitution as a model.

Benjamin Franklin knew about the Iroquois system and its leaders. As the official printer for the Pennsylvania colony, he printed the minutes, or detailed records, of their meetings. His interest in Indians moved the Pennsylvania colony to appoint him as its first Indian commissioner. In his work, he learned that the Iroquois Constitution contained a ban on the forced entry by the government into citizens' homes and a way to remove corrupt leaders from office. He also discovered that the Iroquois Constitution made sure that elected officials remained servants of the people

▲▼▲▼▲▼▲▼▲▼▲▼▲▼▲▼▲▼▲▼▲▼▲▼▲▼▲

POLITICAL CAUCUSES

Caucus, a word for a closed-door political meeting often held to discuss strategy, was first used by English speakers in 1773. It comes from the Algonquian word *caucauasu*, which means "counselor."

▼▲▼▲▼▲▼▲▼▲▼▲▼▲▼▲▼▲▼▲▼▲▼▲▼▲▼

who had chosen them. The Iroquois Constitution set up a system made up of two bodies of lawmakers. This is called a bicameral legislature. Each year, the leader of the Iroquois League had to give a report to the representatives of the Iroquois League.

Franklin became convinced that the Iroquois form of government was better than those of Europe. In 1754 he asked colonial delegates at the Albany Congress to follow the example of the Iroquois when they drew up the Articles of Confederation. The Articles of Confederation were later replaced by the U.S. Constitution.

However, when colonial leaders wrote the U.S. Constitution in 1787, they kept many of these ideas. A constitution is a group of basic rules that govern a country. On September 16, 1987, the U.S. Senate passed a resolution officially stating that the U.S. Constitution was modeled after the Iroquois Constitution.

The ultimate goal of the Iroquois Constitution was peace, but it also gave instructions for conducting war after all peace attempts had failed. Much later, these principles of the Iroquois Constitution were used as a model for the League of Nations, which was formed in 1920 after World War I ended. This organization later became the model for the United Nations.

Leaders and Decisions

Leaders of Indian tribes throughout North America were chosen by consensus. Consensus is the practice of making a choice based on the agreement of all members of the group. Many tribes had a war leader, or chief, whose job it was to keep people from being attacked and to lead warriors against enemies. Another chief kept the daily activities of the tribe running smoothly and helped people settle arguments when they arose.

Indian leaders did not give orders and command people to carry them out. Instead they led by setting a good example. When decisions that affected the whole tribe needed to be made, the leader called for a council meeting. Every tribe had its own rules for who could attend these meetings and how they were run. Often, respected elders and the leaders of smaller family groups that made up the tribe attended. In small tribes, everyone attended meetings. Council meetings often lasted until everyone there had a chance to speak and everyone had reached agreement. This way of making decisions used the wisdom of all members and created a sense of community.

Women's Rights

Many American Indian tribes of the Northeast gave far more respect and power to women than European colonists did. Among the Iroquois tribes, women were the leaders of the longhouses where they lived. They were responsible for farming and for ceremonies. The men in these tribes were responsible for hunting, war, and relations between their tribe and other tribes. Men and women had different roles, but they were considered to be equally valuable. Although men made the decisions for the Iroquois League, women leaders had the power to veto them. A veto is the right to reject a decision. Women could also appoint men to positions of leadership within the Iroquois League.

Women of many North American Indian tribes in addition to the Iroquois tribes had rights that white women did not. Some of the rights that these women had were the right to divorce if they were unhappy in their marriages and the right to control their own possessions. Women also had a right to personal safety. American Indian women sometimes served as spokespersons for their people. European colonists did not believe that women could be leaders, so they would only talk to men about important matters.

▲▼▲▼▲▼▲▼▲▼▲▼▲▼▲▼▲▼▲▼▲▼▲▼▲▼▲▼▲

WOMEN'S RIGHT TO VOTE

Elizabeth Cady Stanton, Lucretia Mott, and Matilda Joslyn Gage were women's rights advocates who worked to obtain the right to vote for all women in the United States. All three knew women from Iroquois League tribes and were influenced by the ideas of these Indian women about the role of women. The U.S. Congress passed the 19th Amendment to the U.S. Constitution in 1920 giving women in the United States the right to vote.

▼▲▼▲▼▲▼▲▼▲▼▲▼▲▼▲▼▲▼▲▼▲▼▲▼▲▼▲▼

AZTEC GOVERNMENT OF MESOAMERICA

Because the Aztec (Mexica) had many people living in the large city of Tenochtitlán, they needed a different form of government. Tenochtitlán was divided into districts. Family leaders voted on Aztec lords to rule the districts. The Aztec emperor confirmed them to office. Leaders of smaller villages and towns were chosen this way as well. Later when the population increased even more, the leaders were chosen by a small group of people with high status. By the time the Spaniards conquered the Aztec, only the emperor and the top four nobles beneath him were chosen by the people. The emperor selected the leaders of districts, towns, and villages.

The people in Tenochtitlán paid taxes, or tributes, to the government in the form of goods and services. These taxes fed and clothed the nobles and government workers. They were also used for building temples and government buildings. Men were required to serve in the army. Other ways to pay taxes were through farming, building, weaving, keeping the city clean, and acting as servants for the emperor and his nobles.

Diplomacy and Treaties

The Aztec expanded their empire very quickly. When they wanted to control another city-state, they sent an ambassador with gifts. This diplomat asked the city-state's ruler to pay tribute. If the ruler did not agree, diplomats visited again to demand that the city-state submit to Aztec rule. To refuse meant war. Many surrendered. Once this happened, the Aztec made a written treaty stating the amount of tribute, or goods and services that the city-state was expected to pay to the Aztec government. Diplomats from both sides held meetings to negotiate these amounts.

The emperor appointed a member of the Aztec nobility, often one of his relatives, to rule the people of the new part of the empire. Apart from this change and that of working to produce goods and to pay the tribute, the people of the former city-states continued to live in much the same way as they had before.

Laws and Courts

One of the first laws that the Aztec established required that farmers plant corn and squash by the side of the roads to feed the poor. The Aztec also had laws against assault, stealing, and being drunk in public. Talking against the emperor was a crime as well.

Local judges in the districts heard most of the cases dealing with lawbreaking. They also heard cases involving disputes over land. The judges called court sessions and listened to the accused, the accuser, and witnesses. If judges took bribes, they were removed from office. Aztec people who went to court had attorneys to represent them. If people were dissatisfied with a judge's ruling, they could appeal their case to a higher court. If they still did not agree with that judge's ruling, they could plead their case before the emperor.

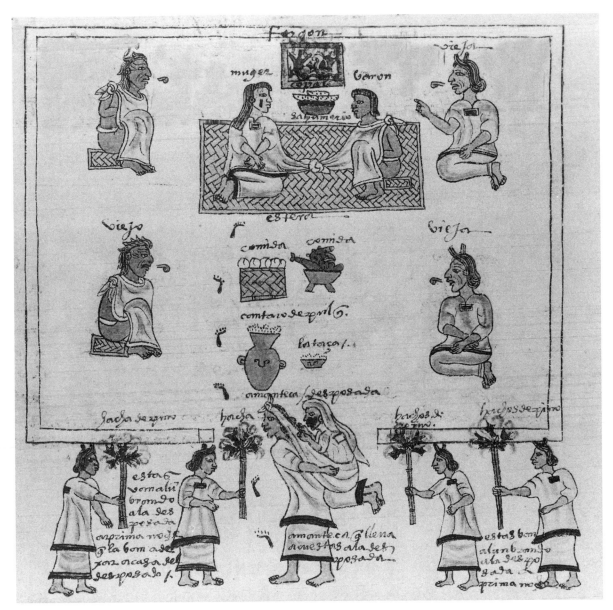

This copy of a picture shows an Aztec marriage ceremony. It is from *Historia de las cosas de Nuevo España* by Bernardo Sahagún. Couples could obtain a legal divorce to end their marriage. *(Library of Congress, Prints and Photographs Division [LC-USZ62-31950])*

The Aztec punished lawbreakers harshly. The death penalty was used for offenses such as stealing, being drunk in public, and lying in court. Because of this, people tended to obey the law. The conquistadores noted that even though Aztec houses had no doors, the people who lived inside of them did not need to worry about their possessions because theft was very rare.

Public Education

All Aztec young people between the ages of 10 and 20 received formal schooling. Most boys lived at schools called *telpochcalli,* which meant "youth's house" in *Nahuatl,* the Aztec language. Girls attended these schools during the day. Boys and girls were taught separately. Both received training in singing, dancing, and music. Boys learned to give speeches and took military training.

Children of nobles attended schools connected to a large temple. Promising youth from the lower classes were also selected to attend these special schools. They were trained to be priests, military officers, and government officials. Students were taught arts, military skills, religion, and astronomy. In addition to hands-on learning, students studied from textbooks.

▲▽▲▽▲▽▲▽▲▽▲▽▲▽▲▽▲▽▲▽▲▽▲▽▲▽▲▽

LEARNING MANNERS

The Spanish priest Father Diego Duran observed Aztec schools in the 1500s. He wrote that students were taught "to be well-mannered, to respect their elders, to serve, to obey, given papers on how they were to serve their lords, to move among them and be polite to them."

▽▲▽▲▽▲▽▲▽▲▽▲▽▲▽▲▽▲▽▲▽▲▽▲▽▲▽▲▽

INCA GOVERNMENT OF SOUTH AMERICA

The Inca, like the Aztec, expanded their empire quickly. They began as bands of farmers and llama herders in an Andean mountain valley until the 1300s, when they expanded their territory. One hundred years later, the Inca had developed a well-organized government. Their empire grew to encompass what is now Peru and what are now parts of Ecuador, Bolivia, and Chile.

The Inca emperor was the supreme ruler of all the people in his empire. Beneath him were a group of nobles who did the day-to-day work involved in ruling the empire. They were not elected. Most had inherited their positions. The Inca emperor appointed others. The Inca had a system of courts as well.

Diplomacy

Like the Aztec, the Inca sent ambassadors with gifts to try to convince rulers of other territories to submit to their rule. Many volunteered to join the Inca Empire, but others fought the Inca army. When the Inca conquered new territory, they built an army outpost there and allowed a loyal member of a local family to rule. Although the people were considered part of the Inca Empire, they were allowed to keep their culture and their customs. When people rebelled, the Inca moved them to another part of the empire. This stopped the rebellion without bloodshed.

Taxes

The oldest tax system in the Americas began in about 2000 B.C. in the Andean Mountains of South America. It required people to perform work as a form of tribute. Under the Inca, this tax system was called a *mit'a*. Every common citizen of the empire was required to pay

WHAT *INCA* MEANS

Although the people who formed the huge empire based in the Andes are called the Inca today, they called themselves the Tahuantinsuyu, which means "the land of four quarters." This is because they divided their empire into four quarters in order to run it more efficiently. They also divided these quarters into smaller districts. *Inca* was the name given to their ruler and his descendants.

LABOR LAWS

Gold mining was a way that some people paid their *mit'a* requirement. In many cases the gold deposits were high in the mountains where the climate was harsh. According to Inca law, sick miners were required to be returned home. Another law required that the miner only work during warm summer months. While in the mining camps, the workers had designated rest periods.

work taxes. The work that people did for the Inca government included farming, building roads, bridges and buildings, running messages, weaving and sewing, and many other tasks.

In addition to allowing the Inca to construct cities and roads, their tax system also allowed them to create a social welfare system. As new territory was brought under their rule, Inca officials took regular counts of the number of people in each district. They made these censuses in order to set the *mit'a* for the district. The Inca were careful never to demand more than people could afford to give. They found out who was widowed, who was poor, and who could not pay taxes. These people were given food. Disabled people were given jobs that they could do, such as shelling corn for the blind. So were old people and children. Everyone in the Inca Empire worked for the common good. Because the Inca made sure that no one under their rule went hungry or homeless, their subjects were loyal.

Laws and Courts

Fancy embroidered clothing, jewelry, or gold were illegal for common people to own. Only the Inca nobility could own or wear those items. Inspectors were allowed to come into people's homes to see if they had any forbidden items. They also checked on people's cleanliness. People who committed crimes were sent before judges. It was very important to the Inca that their judges be fair. According to the law, if a judge took a bribe, that judge was sentenced to death.

Education

Girls who showed special talents were selected as "chosen women" at the age of 10. They were brought to Cuzco, the Inca capital, to learn cooking, weaving, spinning, and other domestic arts, as well as religion. After this training, the Inca emperor decided whether they would be placed to work in a temple or work in his palace.

Cuzco also had four-year schools for the sons of nobility. Here students learned a wide range of subjects, including astronomy, music, philosophy, history, religion, martial arts, poetry, and government. Students also learned how to store and read information using quipus. A quipu is a counting and information-recording device made of knotted string.

GLOSSARY OF ANCIENT CULTURES OF THE AMERICAS

 This glossary lists some of the important cultures, empires, and city-states in the Americas before 1492. Many of them existed hundreds or thousands of years before Europeans arrived in the Americas. Archaeologists try to piece together the history of America's ancient people from their buildings and the smaller objects they left behind. They can only make educated guesses based on the artifacts that they find.

The history of ancient America is one of changes. Because of this, modern people often mistakenly think that entire groups of ancient Indian people disappeared. Indian people and their civilizations did not vanish. Governments rose to power, fell, and were replaced by other governments. Sometimes large groups of people moved. They shared ideas with their neighbors and borrowed ideas from them. The Indians who made up civilizations of the past are the ancestors of the Indians of the Americas who are alive today.

Adena The Adena culture arose along the valleys of the Mississippi and Ohio Rivers and lasted from about 1500 B.C. to A.D. 200. Adena people were farmers and built burial mounds. The Hopewell people followed them.

Anasazi The Anasazi lived in the southwestern part of what is now the United States in New Mexico, Arizona, Utah, and Colorado. Their culture flourished from about 350 B.C. to

A.D. 1450. They are thought to be the ancestors of modern Pueblo people.

Aztec (Mexica)   The Aztec moved into the Valley of Mexico from the north in about A.D. 1100. Their culture followed that of the Toltec in the region. By 1350 they had expanded their empire and became the dominant state in what became central Mexico. They were the powerful group in that area when the Spaniards arrived. At its largest, the main Aztec city of Tenochtitlán had about 250,000 residents.

Chalchihuite   The Chalchihuite people entered what is now the Sierra Madre of Mexico between A.D. 900 and 1250. They were colonized by the Aztec after the Aztec Empire rose to power. They lived in what was considered the northern frontier of the Aztec Empire.

Chavin   Chavin culture flourished in the fertile river valleys of what is now Peru from about 1000 B.C. to about 200 B.C. The Chavin lived about 1,200 to 2,000 years before the Inca Empire was established.

Chimu   The Chimu civilization lasted from 1100 A.D. to the mid-1400s in what is now Peru. The Chimu state was conquered by the Inca.

Chinchorro   The Chinchorro culture, on the coast of what is now Peru, began in about 5000 B.C. It reached its peak in about 3000 B.C. The Chinchorro are best known for the elaborate ways in which they mummified their dead. They are one of the most ancient cultures to have lived in the region.

Hohokam   The Hohokam culture arose in what is now central and southern Arizona in about 300 B.C. Hohokam people are thought to be the ancestors of the Akimel O'odham (Pima) and the Tohono O'odham (Papago). The Hohokam lived in the Southwest in the same time period as the Anasazi. Their settlements were south of those of the Anasazi.

Hopewell   Hopewell culture arose along the valleys of the Mississippi and Ohio Rivers in about 300 B.C. The Hopewell are considered part of the Mound Builders, along with the Adena people who came before them. They built huge earthworks and flourished until about A.D. 700. They were followed by the Mississippian Culture.

Inca   The Inca established an empire in what is now Peru in about A.D. 1000 and rapidly expanded it. This empire extended from what is now northwest Argentina to parts of what is now Colombia. The Inca Empire was in power when the Spanish conquistador Francisco Pizarro arrived in South America.

Iroquois League (Haudenosaunee)   The Iroquois League, or Haudenosaunee, was an alliance of Northeast tribes established some time between A.D. 1000 and 1400. The tribes included the Oneida, Mohawk, Cayuga, Onondaga, Seneca, and later the Tuscarora.

Maya   The Maya civilization arose in what is now the Yucatán Peninsula of Mexico starting in about 1500 B.C. They did not have a centralized government but instead formed city-states. Maya people also lived in what are now Belize, Guatemala, El Salvador, and Honduras. When the Aztec expanded their empire, they began collecting taxes from the Maya and demanded loyalty to the Aztec Emperor.

Mississippian Culture   The Mississippian Culture arose in about A.D. 1000. Sometimes these people are called temple mound builders. Unlike the Adena and Hopewell people, they built earthworks for temples and ceremonial centers, rather than for burials. They built Cahokia, a city of about 30,000 people, near what is St. Louis, Missouri, today. Mississippian Culture started to weaken in the 1500s, but early French explorers encountered some temple mound builders in the late 1600s.

Mixtec   The Mixtec lived in what is now southern Mexico. Their culture arose in about A.D. 900. The Aztec Empire eventually dominated the Mixtec city-states, but their culture continued to thrive until the arrival of the Spaniards.

Moche   The Moche culture arose on the northern coast of what is now Peru in about 200 B.C. It flourished until about A.D. 600. The Moche were master artists.

Mound Builders   These were American Indians of several cultures who lived in the Mississippi and Ohio River Valleys over a period of time. Some Mound Builders also lived in the Southeast. These people of the Adena, Hopewell, and Mississippian cultures built extensive earthworks.

Nazca   The Nazca people lived in the lowlands of what is now Peru. Their culture arose starting in about 600 B.C. and lasted until about A.D. 900. Later the area where they lived became part of the Inca Empire.

Old Copper Culture   Peoples who lived from about 4000 B.C. to 1500 B.C. in the Great Lakes region of North America. These Indians worked with copper deposits that were close to the surface of the Earth. They made some of the earliest metal tools and objects in the world.

Olmec   The Olmec culture flourished starting in about 1700 B.C. in the coastal lowlands of what is now Mexico. It lasted until about 400 B.C. The Olmec built several cities, including La Venta, which had a population of about 18,000. The Olmec are also known as the Rubber People because they made items from rubber.

Paracas   The Paracas culture arose in the river valleys of what is now Peru in about 1300 B.C. and flourished until about A.D. 20. Paracas people invented many weaving and pottery techniques. A thousand years later, the area where they lived became part of the Inca Empire.

Paleo-Indians   A general term for those who lived before about 4000 B.C. They were the oldest peoples of the Americas. They hunted for their food, killing large mammals, such as the wooly mammoth and the mastodon.

Poverty Point Culture   The people of Poverty Point lived in the Lower Mississippi Valley between 1730 and 1350 B.C. They are a small, distinct group within Mississippian, or Mound Building, Culture.

Teotihuacán   The Teotihuacán culture flourished in the central valley of what is now Mexico from about 1000 B.C. to 900 A.D. At its center was the city-state of Teotihuacán, which was at its strongest from about A.D. 1 to about 650. In A.D. 500 the city was home to between 100,000 and 200,000 people.

Thule   The Thule culture arose in what is now northwestern Alaska between 1,000 and 2,000 years ago. Then it spread to Greenland. Thule people were the ancestors of the Inuit. They are known for their tool-making ability.

Toltec   The Toltec migrated into what is now known as the Valley of Mexico in central Mexico in about A.D. 800. They established their capital at Tula in about 900. About 60,000 people lived in Tula. The Toltec rule lasted until some time in the

1100s, when invading groups attacked and overthrew them. Little is known about the Toltec because the Aztec used the ruins of Tula as a source of building materials for their own monuments.

Zapotec   The Zapotec established a city-state south of the Mixtec in what is now southern Mexico. In about 500 B.C. they began building the city of Monte Albán. By A.D. 450, more than 15,000 people lived in Monte Albán. Later this grew to 25,000 people. By about 700 A.D. the Zapotec began moving away from their city. Although their culture remained, the Zapotec no longer had a city-state.

TRIBES ORGANIZED BY CULTURE AREA

North American Culture Areas

ARCTIC CULTURE AREA
Aleut
Inuit

CALIFORNIA CULTURE AREA
Achomawi (Pit River)
Akwaala
Alliklik (Tataviam)
Atsugewi (Pit River)
Bear River
Cahto (Kato)
Cahuilla
Chilula
Chimariko
Chumash
Costanoan (Ohlone)
Cupeño
Diegueño (Ipai)
Esselen
Fernandeño
Gabrieliño
Huchnom
Hupa
Ipai (Diegueño)
Juaneño
Kamia (Tipai)
Karok
Kitanemuk

Konomihu
Lassik
Luiseño
Maidu
Mattole
Miwok
Nicoleño
Nomlaki
Nongatl
Okwanuchu
Patwin (subgroup of Wintun)
Pomo
Salinas
Serrano
Shasta
Sinkyone
Tolowa (Smith River)
Tubatulabal (Kern River)
Vanyume
Wailaki
Wappo
Whilkut
Wintu (subgroup of Wintun)
Wintun
Wiyot
Yahi

Yana
Yokuts
Yuki
Yurok

GREAT BASIN CULTURE AREA
Bannock
Chemehuevi
Kawaiisu
Mono
Paiute
Panamint
Sheepeater (subgroup
of Bannock
and Shoshone)
Shoshone
Snake (subgroup of Paiute)
Ute
Washoe

GREAT PLAINS CULTURE AREA
Arapaho
Arikara
Assiniboine
Atsina (Gros Ventre)
Blackfeet
Blood (subgroup of Blackfeet)
Cheyenne
Comanche
Crow
Hidatsa
Ioway
Kaw
Kichai
Kiowa
Kiowa-Apache
Mandan
Missouria
Omaha
Osage
Otoe
Pawnee
Piegan (subgroup of Blackfeet)

Plains Cree
Plains Ojibway
Ponca
Quapaw
Sarcee
Sioux (Dakota, Lakota, Nakota)
Tawakoni
Tawehash
Tonkawa
Waco
Wichita
Yscani

NORTHEAST CULTURE AREA
Abenaki
Algonkin
Amikwa (Otter)
Cayuga
Chippewa (Ojibway,
Anishinabe)
Chowanoc
Conoy
Coree (Coranine)
Erie
Fox (Mesquaki)
Hatteras
Honniasont
Huron (Wyandot)
Illinois
Iroquois (Haudenosaunee)
Kickapoo
Kitchigami
Lenni Lenape (Delaware)
Machapunga
Mahican
Maliseet
Manhattan (subgroup of Lenni
Lenape or Wappinger)
Massachuset
Mattabesac
Meherrin
Menominee
Miami

Micmac

Mingo (subgroup of Iroquois)

Mohawk

Mohegan

Montauk

Moratok

Nanticoke

Narragansett

Nauset

Neusiok

Neutral (Attiwandaronk)

Niantic

Nipmuc

Noquet

Nottaway

Oneida

Onondaga

Ottawa

Otter (Amikwa)

Pamlico (Pomeiok)

Passamaquoddy

Paugussett

Penacook

Penobscot

Pequot

Pocomtuc

Poospatuck
(subgroup of Montauk)

Potawatomi

Powhatan

Raritan
(subgroup of Lenni Lenape)

Roanoke

Sac

Sakonnet

Secotan

Seneca

Shawnee

Shinnecock
(subgroup of Montauk)

Susquehannock

Tobacco (Petun)

Tuscarora

Wampanoag

Wappinger

Weapemeoc

Wenro

Winnebago (Ho-Chunk)

**NORTHWEST COAST
CULTURE AREA**

Ahantchuyuk

Alsea

Atfalati

Bella Coola

Cathlamet

Cathlapotle

Chastacosta

Chehalis

Chelamela

Chepenafa (Mary's River)

Chetco

Chilluckittequaw

Chimakum

Chinook

Clackamas

Clallam

Clatskanie

Clatsop

Clowwewalla

Comox

Coos

Coquille (Mishikhwutmetunne)

Cowichan

Cowlitz

Dakubetede

Duwamish

Gitskan

Haida

Haisla

Heiltsuk

Kalapuya

Kuitsh

Kwakiutl

Kwalhioqua
Latgawa
Luckiamute
Lumni
Makah
Miluk
Muckleshoot
Multomah (Wappato)
Nanaimo
Nisga
Nisqually
Nooksack
Nootka
Puntlatch
Puyallup
Quaitso (Queets)
Quileute
Quinault
Rogue
Sahehwamish
Samish
Santiam
Seechelt
Semiahmoo
Siletz
Siuslaw
Skagit
Skilloot
Skykomish
Snohomish
Snoqualmie
Songish
Squamish
Squaxon (Squaxin)
Stalo
Swallah
Swinomish
Takelma (Rogue)
Taltushtuntude
Tillamook
Tlingit
Tsimshian

Tututni (Rogue)
Twana
Umpqua
Wappato (Multomah)
Wasco
Watlala (Cascade)
Yamel
Yaquina
Yoncalla

PLATEAU CULTURE AREA

Cayuse
Chelan
Coeur d'Alene
Columbia (Sinkiuse)
Colville
Entiat
Flathead (Salish)
Kalispel
Klamath
Klickitat
Kootenai (Flathead)
Lake (Senijextee)
Lillooet
Methow
Modoc
Molalla
Nez Perce
Ntlakyapamuk (Thompson)
Okanagan
Palouse
Pshwanwapam
Sanpoil
Shuswap
Sinkaietk
Sinkakaius
Skin (Tapanash)
Spokan
Stuwihamuk
Taidnapam
Tenino
Tyigh

Umatilla
Walla Walla
Wanapam
Wauyukma
Wenatchee
Wishram
Yakama

SOUTHEAST CULTURE AREA
Acolapissa
Adai
Ais
Akokisa
Alabama
Amacano
Apalachee
Apalachicola
Atakapa
Avoyel
Bayogoula
Bidai
Biloxi
Caddo
Calusa
Caparaz
Cape Fear
Catawba
Chakchiuma
Chatot
Chawasha (subgroup
of Chitimacha)
Cheraw (Sara)
Cherokee
Chiaha
Chickasaw
Chine
Chitimacha
Choctaw
Congaree
Coushatta
Creek
Cusabo
Deadose

Eno
Eyeish (Ayish)
Griga
Guacata
Guale
Hitchiti
Houma
Ibitoupa
Jeaga
Kaskinampo
Keyauwee
Koroa
Lumbee
Manahoac
Miccosukee
(subgroup of Seminole)
Mobile
Monacan
Moneton
Muklasa
Nahyssan
Napochi
Natchez
Occaneechi
Oconee
Ofo
Okelousa
Okmulgee
Opelousa
Osochi
Pasacagoula
Patiri
Pawokti
Pee Dee
Pensacola
Quinipissa
Santee (Issati)
Saponi
Sawokli
Seminole
Sewee
Shakori
Sissipahaw

Sugeree
Taensa
Tamathli
Tangipahoa
Taposa
Tawasa
Tekesta
Timucua
Tiou
Tohome
Tunica
Tuskegee
Tutelo
Waccamaw
Washa (subgroup of
Chitimacha)
Wateree
Waxhaw
Winyaw
Woccon
Yadkin
Yamasee
Yazoo
Yuchi

SOUTHWEST CULTURE AREA
Akimel O'odham (Pima)
Apache
Coahuiltec
Cocopah
Halchidhoma
Halyikwamai
Havasupai
Hopi
Hualapai
Jumano (Shuman)
Karankawa
Keres (Pueblo Indians)
Kohuana
Maricopa
Mojave
Navajo (Dineh)
Piro (Pueblo Indians)

Pueblo
Quenchan (Yuma)
Shuman (Jumano)
Sobaipuri
Tewa (Pueblo Indians)
Tiwa (Pueblo Indians)
Tohono O'odham (Papago)
Towa (Jemez, Pueblo Indians)
Yaqui
Yavapai
Yuma (Quechan)
Zuni

SUBARCTIC CULTURE AREA
Ahtena (Copper)
Beaver (Tsattine)
Beothuk
Carrier
Chilcotin
Chipewyan
Cree
Dogrib
Eyak
Han
Hare (Kawchottine)
Ingalik
Kolchan
Koyukon
Kutchin
Montagnais
Nabesna
Nahane
Naskapi
Sekani
Slave (Slavery,
Etchaottine)
Tahltan
Tanaina
Tanana
Tatsanottine (Yellowknife)
Tsetsaut
Tutchone (Mountain)

Mesoamerican Culture Area*

Aztec (Mexica-Nahuatl)
Chalchiuites
Maya
Mixtec

Olmec
Toltec
Zapotec

Circum-Caribbean Culture Area
(West Indies and Portion of Central America)

Arawak
Boruca
Carib
Ciboney
Ciguayo
Coiba
Corobici
Cuna
Guaymi
Guetar
Jicaque
Lucayo

Matagalpa
Mosquito
Paya
Rama
Silam
Sumo
Taino
Talamanca
Ulva
Voto
Yosco

South American Culture Areas*

ANDEAN CULTURE AREA
Achuari
Aguaruna
Chavin
Chimu
Inca
Jivaro
Mapuche
Moche
Nazca
Quecha

**CENTRAL AND
SOUTHERN CULTURE AREA**
Guarani
Mapuche

**TROPICAL FOREST (AMAZON
BASIN) CULTURE AREA**
Arawak
Carib
Tupi

* These lists do not attempt to include all groups in the area. They do, however, include a mix of ancient and modern peoples.

Appendix
MAPS

North American, Mesoamerican, and Circum-Caribbean Indian Culture Areas

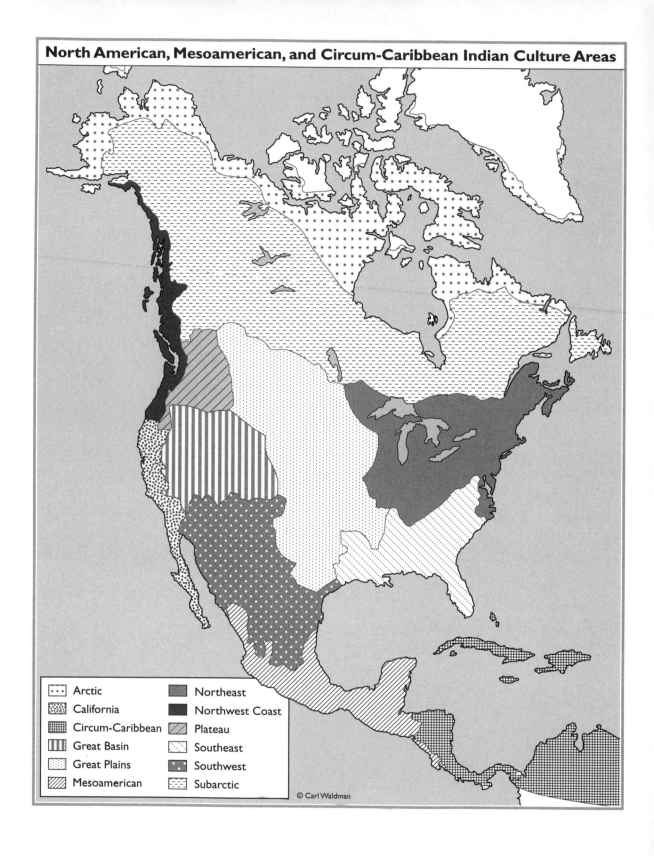

Legend:
- Arctic
- California
- Circum-Caribbean
- Great Basin
- Great Plains
- Mesoamerican
- Northeast
- Northwest Coast
- Plateau
- Southeast
- Southwest
- Subarctic

© Carl Waldman

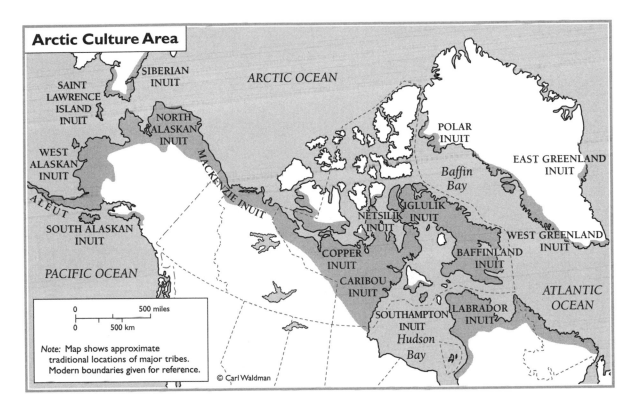

Arctic Culture Area

SIBERIAN INUIT

SAINT LAWRENCE ISLAND INUIT

ARCTIC OCEAN

NORTH ALASKAN INUIT

WEST ALASKAN INUIT

POLAR INUIT

EAST GREENLAND INUIT

Baffin Bay

ALEUT

SOUTH ALASKAN INUIT

MACKENZIE INUIT

NETSILIK INUIT

IGLULIK INUIT

WEST GREENLAND INUIT

PACIFIC OCEAN

COPPER INUIT

BAFFINLAND INUIT

CARIBOU INUIT

ATLANTIC OCEAN

SOUTHAMPTON INUIT

LABRADOR INUIT

Hudson Bay

| 0 | 500 miles |
| 0 | 500 km |

Note: Map shows approximate traditional locations of major tribes. Modern boundaries given for reference.

© Carl Waldman

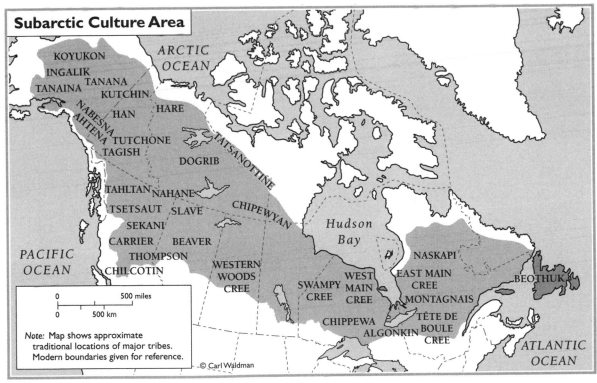

Subarctic Culture Area

KOYUKON

INGALIK

TANANA

TANAINA

KUTCHIN

ARCTIC OCEAN

NABESNA

AHTENA

HAN

HARE

TUTCHONE

TAGISH

TATSANOTTINE

DOGRIB

TAHLTAN

NAHANE

TSETSAUT

SLAVE

CHIPEWYAN

Hudson Bay

SEKANI

CARRIER

BEAVER

NASKAPI

THOMPSON

CHILCOTIN

WESTERN WOODS CREE

EAST MAIN CREE

BEOTHUK

PACIFIC OCEAN

WEST MAIN CREE

SWAMPY CREE

MONTAGNAIS

CHIPPEWA

ALGONKIN

TÊTE DE BOULE CREE

ATLANTIC OCEAN

| 0 | 500 miles |
| 0 | 500 km |

Note: Map shows approximate traditional locations of major tribes. Modern boundaries given for reference.

© Carl Waldman

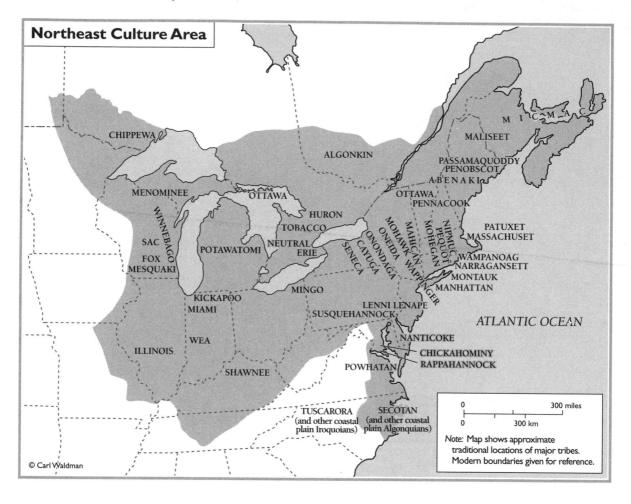

Northeast Culture Area

CHIPPEWA

ALGONKIN

M I C M A C

MALISEET

PASSAMAQUODDY
PENOBSCOT

A B E N A K I

MENOMINEE

OTTAWA

OTTAWA

PENNACOOK

WINNEBAGO

HURON

NIPMUC

PATUXET
MASSACHUSET

TOBACCO

MOHAWK
MAHICAN
PEQUOT
MOHEGAN

SAC

NEUTRAL

ONEIDA

POTAWATOMI

ERIE

ONONDAGA

WAMPANOAG
NARRAGANSETT

FOX
MESQUAKI

CAYUGA

SENECA

WAPPINGER

MONTAUK
MANHATTAN

MINGO

KICKAPOO

LENNI LENAPE

MIAMI

SUSQUEHANNOCK

ATLANTIC OCEAN

WEA

NANTICOKE

ILLINOIS

CHICKAHOMINY
RAPPAHANNOCK

SHAWNEE

POWHATAN

TUSCARORA
(and other coastal
plain Iroquoians)

SECOTAN
(and other coastal
plain Algonquians)

0   300 miles
0   300 km

Note: Map shows approximate
traditional locations of major tribes.
Modern boundaries given for reference.

© Carl Waldman

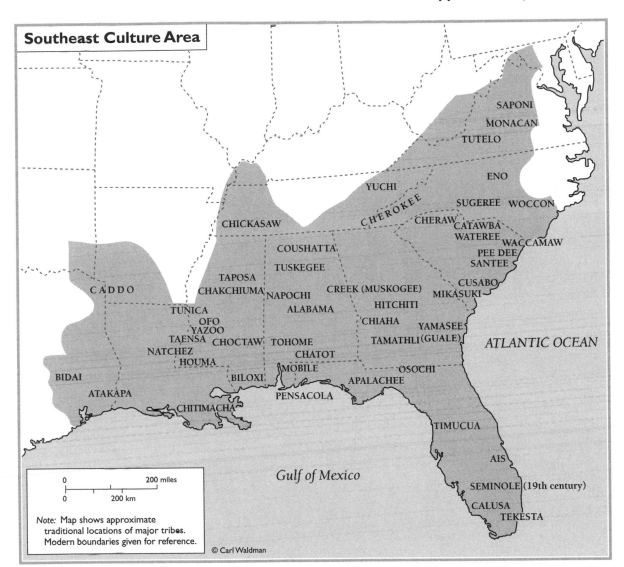

Southeast Culture Area

SAPONI
MONACAN
TUTELO

ENO

YUCHI

SUGEREE   WOCCON

CHEROKEE

CHERAW   CATAWBA
WATEREE   WACCAMAW

CHICKASAW

PEE DEE
SANTEE

COUSHATTA

TUSKEGEE

CUSABO

TAPOSA
CHAKCHIUMA

NAPOCHI

CREEK (MUSKOGEE)   MIKASUKI

CADDO

ALABAMA

HITCHITI

TUNICA
OFO
YAZOO
TAENSA   CHOCTAW   TOHOME
NATCHEZ
HOUMA

CHIAHA

YAMASEE

TAMATHLI (GUALE)

ATLANTIC OCEAN

CHATOT

OSOCHI

BIDAI

BILOXI   MOBILE

APALACHEE

ATAKAPA

PENSACOLA

CHITIMACHA

TIMUCUA

AIS

Gulf of Mexico

SEMINOLE (19th century)

CALUSA
TEKESTA

0   200 miles

0   200 km

Note: Map shows approximate
traditional locations of major tribes.
Modern boundaries given for reference.

© Carl Waldman

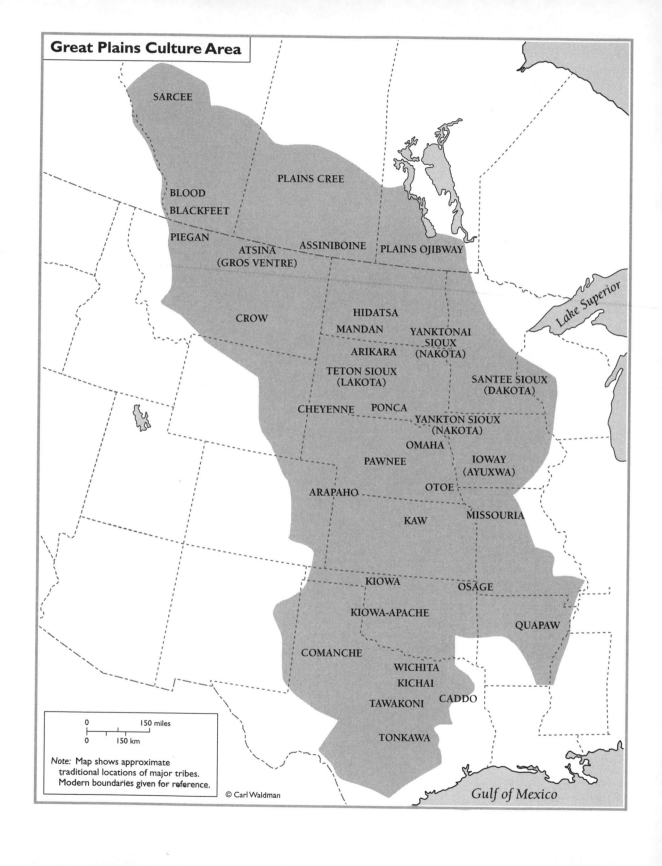

Great Plains Culture Area

SARCEE

PLAINS CREE

BLOOD
BLACKFEET
PIEGAN
ATSINA
(GROS VENTRE)

ASSINIBOINE

PLAINS OJIBWAY

Lake Superior

CROW

HIDATSA
MANDAN
ARIKARA
TETON SIOUX
(LAKOTA)

YANKTONAI
SIOUX
(NAKOTA)

SANTEE SIOUX
(DAKOTA)

CHEYENNE

PONCA

YANKTON SIOUX
(NAKOTA)

OMAHA

PAWNEE

IOWAY
(AYUXWA)

ARAPAHO

OTOE

KAW

MISSOURIA

KIOWA

OSAGE

KIOWA-APACHE

QUAPAW

COMANCHE

WICHITA
KICHAI
TAWAKONI

CADDO

TONKAWA

0   150 miles
0   150 km

Note: Map shows approximate
traditional locations of major tribes.
Modern boundaries given for reference.

© Carl Waldman

Gulf of Mexico

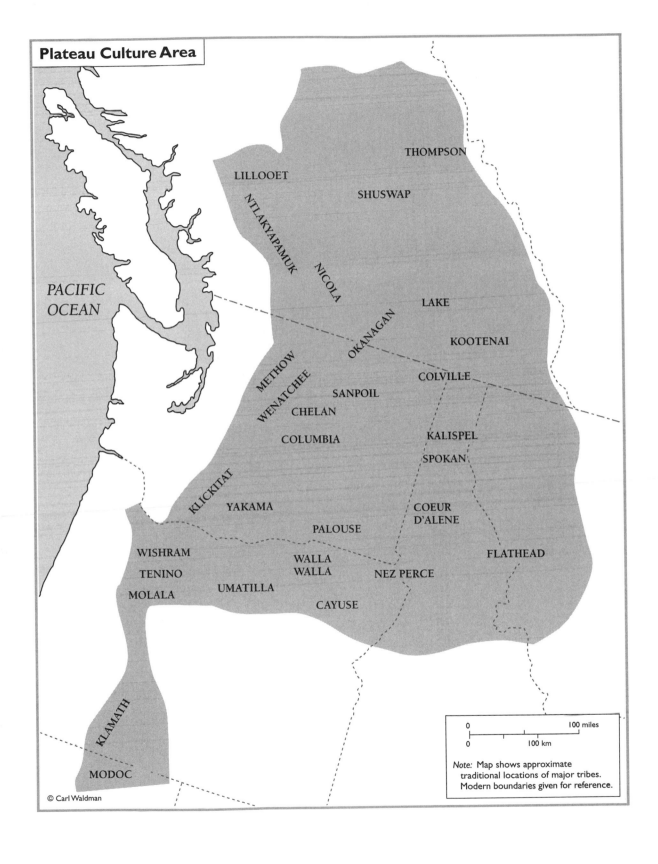

Plateau Culture Area

PACIFIC
OCEAN

THOMPSON

LILLOOET

SHUSWAP

NTLAKYAPAMUK

NICOLA

LAKE

OKANAGAN

KOOTENAI

METHOW

COLVILLE

WENATCHEE

SANPOIL

CHELAN

KALISPEL

COLUMBIA

SPOKAN

KLICKITAT

YAKAMA

COEUR
D'ALENE

PALOUSE

WISHRAM

FLATHEAD

WALLA
WALLA

TENINO

NEZ PERCE

MOLALA

UMATILLA

CAYUSE

KLAMATH

MODOC

© Carl Waldman

0   100 miles

0   100 km

Note: Map shows approximate
traditional locations of major tribes.
Modern boundaries given for reference.

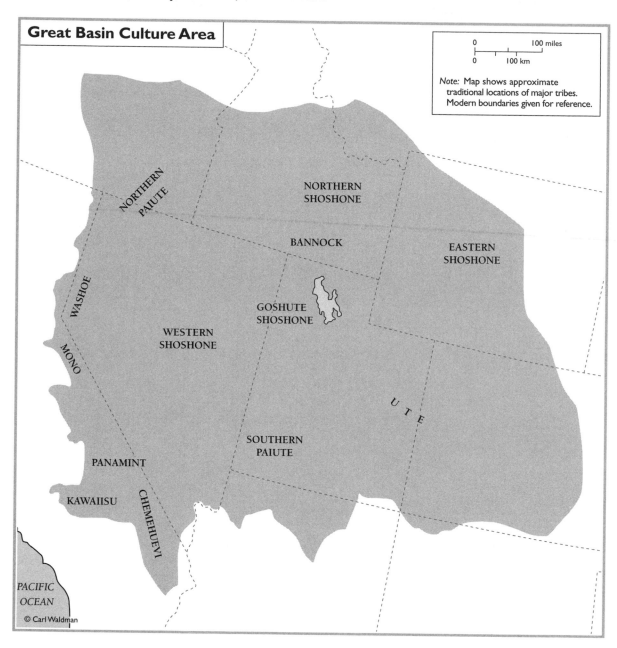

Great Basin Culture Area

0   100 miles
0   100 km

Note: Map shows approximate traditional locations of major tribes. Modern boundaries given for reference.

NORTHERN PAIUTE

NORTHERN SHOSHONE

BANNOCK

EASTERN SHOSHONE

WASHOE

GOSHUTE SHOSHONE

WESTERN SHOSHONE

MONO

U T E

SOUTHERN PAIUTE

PANAMINT

KAWAIISU

CHEMEHUEVI

PACIFIC OCEAN

© Carl Waldman

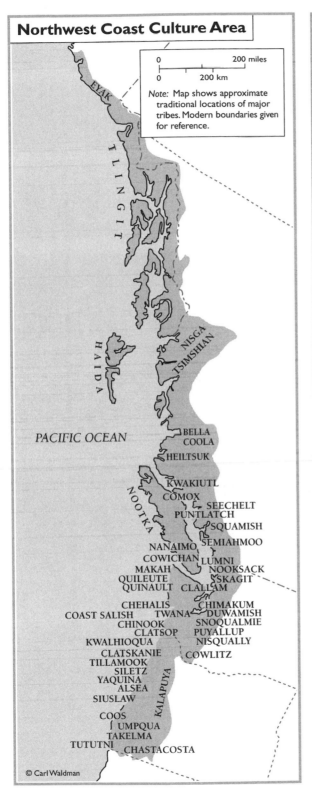

Northwest Coast Culture Area

0   200 miles
0   200 km

Note: Map shows approximate
traditional locations of major
tribes. Modern boundaries given
for reference.

EYAK

TLINGIT

HAIDA

NISGA
TSIMSHIAN

PACIFIC OCEAN

BELLA
COOLA
HEILTSUK
KWAKIUTL
COMOX
SEECHELT
PUNTLATCH
SQUAMISH
NOOTKA
SEMIAHMOO
NANAIMO
COWICHAN   LUMNI
MAKAH   NOOKSACK
QUILEUTE   SKAGIT
QUINAULT   CLALLAM
CHEHALIS   CHIMAKUM
COAST SALISH   TWANA   DUWAMISH
CHINOOK   SNOQUALMIE
CLATSOP   PUYALLUP
KWALHIOQUA   NISQUALLY
CLATSKANIE   COWLITZ
TILLAMOOK
SILETZ
YAQUINA
ALSEA
SIUSLAW
COOS
UMPQUA
TAKELMA
TUTUTNI   CHASTACOSTA

KALAPUYA

© Carl Waldman

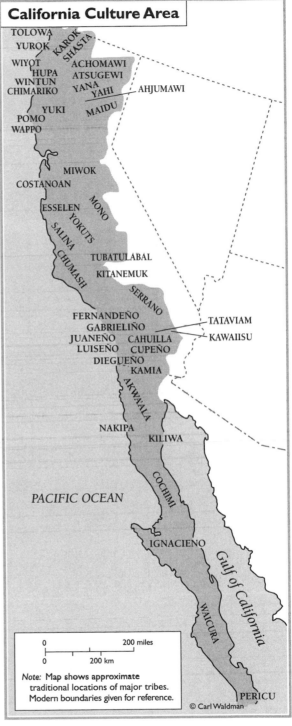

California Culture Area

TOLOWA
YUROK   KAROK   SHASTA
WIYOT   ACHOMAWI
HUPA   ATSUGEWI
WINTUN   YANA
CHIMARIKO   YAHI
       AHJUMAWI
YUKI   MAIDU
POMO
WAPPO

MIWOK
COSTANOAN

ESSELEN
   MONO
  YOKUTS
SALINA
CHUMASH   TUBATULABAL
    KITANEMUK
     SERRANO

FERNANDEÑO
GABRIELIÑO   TATAVIAM
JUANEÑO   CAHUILLA
LUISEÑO   CUPEÑO   KAWAIISU
DIEGUEÑO
   KAMIA
AKWA'ALA

NAKIPA
   KILIWA

PACIFIC OCEAN

COCHIMI

IGNACIENO

Gulf of California

WAICURA

PERICU

0   200 miles
0   200 km

Note: Map shows approximate
traditional locations of major tribes.
Modern boundaries given for reference.

© Carl Waldman

Southwest Culture Area

HUALAPAI

HAVASUPAI

HOPI

MOJAVE

NAVAJO

JICARILLA
APACHE

HALCHIDHOMA

YAVAPAI

TIWA

TOWA TEWA

MARICOPA

ZUNI

PECOS

YUMA

KERES

COCOPAH

PIRO

TIWA

TOHONO
O'ODHAM

WESTERN
APACHE

MIMBRENO
APACHE

CHIRICAHUA
APACHE

MESCALERO
APACHE

AKIMEL
O'ODHAM

SUMA

OPATA

JUMANO

SERI

CAHITA

JOVA

CONCHO

LIPAN
APACHE

Gulf of California

YAQUI

TARAHUMARA

KARANKAWA

TEPAHUE

VAVROHIO

TOBOSO

MAYO

ZOE

COMANITO

NIO

COAHUILTEC

LAGUNERO

GUASAVE

TEPEHUAN

ZACATEC

BOCALOS

JANAMBRE

PISONES

TAMAULIPEC

Gulf
of
Mexico

NEGRITO

PACIFIC OCEAN

HUICHOL

TEPECANO

GUACHICHIL

JONAZ

COLOTLAN

GUAMARES

TEUL

PAME

| 0 | | 150 miles |
| 0 | | 150 km |

Note: Map shows approximate
traditional locations of major tribes.
Modern boundaries given for reference.

© Carl Waldman

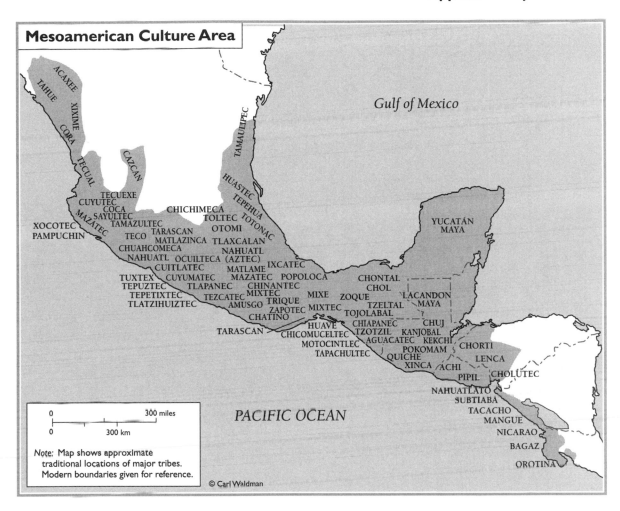

Mesoamerican Culture Area

Gulf of Mexico

PACIFIC OCEAN

ACAXEE
TAHUE
XIXIME
CORA
TECUAL
CAZCAN
TECUEXE
CUYUTEC
COCA
SAYULTEC
XOCOTEC
PAMPUCHIN
MAZATEC
TAMAZULTEC
TARASCAN
TECO
MATLAZINCA
CHUAHCOMECA
NAHUATL
NAHUATL
OCUILTECA (AZTEC)
CUITLATEC
TUXTEX
CUYUMATEC
TEPUZTEC
TLAPANEC
TEPETIXTEC
TEZCATEC
MIXTEC
TLATZIHUIZTEC
AMUSGO
TRIQUE
CHATINO
TARASCAN
CHICOMUCELTEC
MOTOCINTLEC
TAPACHULTEC

CHICHIMECA
TOLTEC
OTOMI
TLAXCALAN
MATLAME
IXCATEC
MAZATEC
POPOLOCA
CHINANTEC
ZAPOTEC
MIXTEC
HUAVE

TAMAULIPEC
HUASTEC
TEPEHUA
TOTONAC

MIXE
ZOQUE

CHONTAL
CHOL
TZELTAL
TOJOLABAL
CHIAPANEC
TZOTZIL
AGUACATEC
QUICHE
XINCA
ACHI
PIPIL

YUCATÁN
MAYA

LACANDON
MAYA

CHUJ
KANJOBAL
KEKCHI
POKOMAM
CHORTI
LENCA
CHOLUTEC

NAHUATLATO
SUBTIABA
TACACHO
MANGUE
NICARAO
BAGAZ
OROTINA

0   300 miles
0   300 km

Note: Map shows approximate
traditional locations of major tribes.
Modern boundaries given for reference.

© Carl Waldman

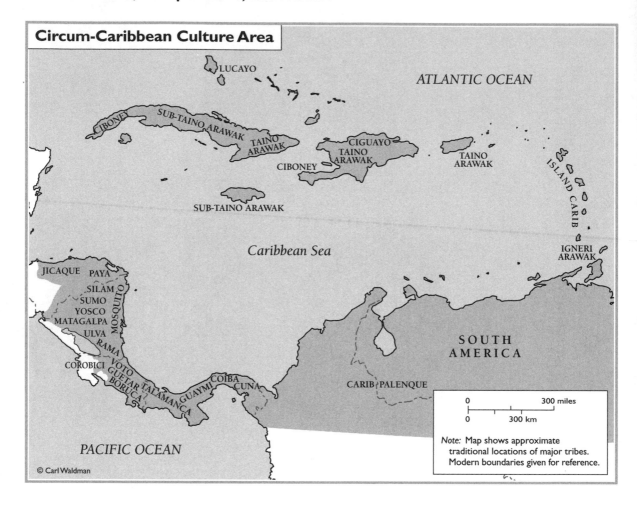

Circum-Caribbean Culture Area

LUCAYO

ATLANTIC OCEAN

CIBONEY

SUB-TAINO ARAWAK

TAINO ARAWAK

CIBONEY

CIGUAYO TAINO ARAWAK

TAINO ARAWAK

ISLAND CARIB

SUB-TAINO ARAWAK

IGNERI ARAWAK

Caribbean Sea

JICAQUE   PAYA

SILAM

SUMO

YOSCO

MATAGALPA

ULVA

RAMA

COROBICI

VOTO

GUETAR TALAMANCA

BORUCA

MOSQUITO

GUAYMI

COIBA

CUNA

SOUTH AMERICA

CARIB PALENQUE

0   300 miles

0   300 km

Note: Map shows approximate traditional locations of major tribes. Modern boundaries given for reference.

PACIFIC OCEAN

© Carl Waldman

South American Culture Areas

CIRCUM-CARIBBEAN

CARIB
PALENQUE

TUPI
ARAWAK

AGUARUNA
ACHUARI
JIVARO

CARIB

ARAWAK

TUPI

CHIMU

INCA

TROPICAL FOREST

ANDEAN

EASTERN
HIGHLANDS

GUARANI

GUARANI

CENTRAL AND SOUTHERN

MAPUCHE

PAMPAS

TIERRA DEL FUEGO

ANDEAN   Culture areas

PAMPAS   Regions

MAPUCHE   Tribes and peoples

————   Approximate culture area boundaries

·········   Approximate regional boundaries

0   800 miles

0   800 km

Note: See the Circum-Caribbean map for the entire scope of the culture area.

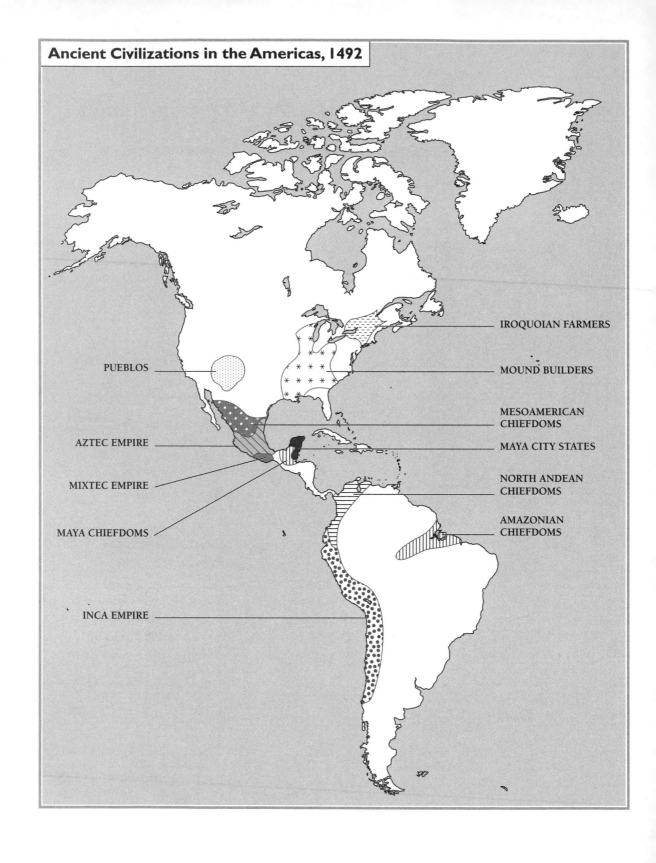

Ancient Civilizations in the Americas, 1492

IROQUOIAN FARMERS

PUEBLOS

MOUND BUILDERS

MESOAMERICAN
CHIEFDOMS

AZTEC EMPIRE

MAYA CITY STATES

MIXTEC EMPIRE

NORTH ANDEAN
CHIEFDOMS

MAYA CHIEFDOMS

AMAZONIAN
CHIEFDOMS

INCA EMPIRE

FURTHER READING

Baquedano, Elizabeth. *Aztec, Inca and Maya.* New York: DK Publishing, 2000.

Carrasco, David. *Daily Life of the Aztecs: Keepers of the Sun and Moon.* Westport, Conn.: Greenwood Press, 1998.

Durrett, Deanne. *Unsung Heroes of World War II: The Story of the Navajo Code Talkers.* New York: Facts On File, Inc., 1998.

Goodchild, Peter. *Survival Skills of the North American Indians.* 2d ed. Chicago: Chicago Review Press, 1999.

Keoke, Emory, and Kay Marie Porterfield. *The Encyclopedia of American Indian Contributions to the World: 15,000 Years of Inventions and Innovation.* New York: Facts On File, Inc., 2002.

Liptak, Karen. *North American Indian Survival Skills.* New York: Franklin Watts, 1990.

Lourie, Peter. *Lost Treasure of the Inca.* Honesdale, Pa.: Boyds Mills Press, 1999.

Malpass, Michael A. *Daily Life in the Inca Empire.* Westport, Conn.: Greenwood Press, 2002.

Montgomery, David. *Native American Crafts and Skills: A Fully Illustrated Guide to Wilderness Living and Survival.* Guilford, Conn.: The Lyons Press, 2000.

Murdoch, David. *Eyewitness: North American Indians.* New York: DK Publishers, 2000.

Nardo, Don. *The Native Americans (History of Weapons and Warfare).* Farmington Hills, Mich: Lucent Books, 2002.

Sharer, Robert J. *Daily Life in Maya Civilization.* Westport, Conn.: Greenwood Press, 2002.

Steedman, Scott. *How Would You Survive As an American Indian?* New York: Franklin Watts, 1997.

Steele, Philip. *The Aztec News.* Cambridge, Mass.: Candlewick Press, 2000.

Taylor, Colin F. *Native American Weapons*. University of Oklahoma Press, 2001.

Wolfson, Evelyn. *From Abenaki to Zuni: A Dictionary of Native American Tribes*. New York: Walker Publishing Co., Inc., 1988.

Wood, Marian. *Ancient America: Cultural Atlas for Young People, Revised Edition*. New York: Facts On File, Inc., 2003.

INDEX

Page numbers in *italics* indicate photographs. Page numbers in **boldface** indicate box features. Page numbers followed by *m* indicate maps. Page numbers followed by *g* indicate glossary entries. Page numbers followed by *t* indicate time line entries.